Heaven's perspective

Revelation

by Tim Chester

Revelation For You

If you are reading *Revelation For You* (see page 77) alongside this Good Book Guide, here is how the studies in this booklet link to the chapters of *Revelation For You*:

Study One → Ch 1
Study Two → Ch 2
Study Three → Ch 3
Study Four → Ch 4-5

Study Five → Ch 6-7
Study Six → Ch 8-9
Study Seven → Ch 9-10

Heaven's perspective
The Good Book Guide to Revelation
© Tim Chester/The Good Book Company, 2019. Reprinted 2021.
Series Consultants: Tim Chester, Tim Thornborough,
Anne Woodcock, Carl Laferton

Published by:
The Good Book Company

thegoodbook.com | thegoodbook.co.uk
thegoodbook.com.au | thegoodbook.co.nz | thegoodbook.co.in

ISBN: 9781910307021

Printed in India

CONTENTS

Introduction: Good Book Guides

Every Bible-study group is different—yours may take place in a church building, in a home or in a cafe, on a train, over a leisurely mid-morning coffee or squashed into a 30-minute lunch break. Your group may include new Christians, mature Christians, non-Christians, mothers with children, students, business people or teens. That's why we've designed these *Good Book Guides* to be flexible for use in many different situations.

Our aim in each session is to uncover the meaning of a passage, and see how it fits into the "big picture" of the Bible. But that can never be the end. We also need to appropriately apply what we have discovered to our lives. Let's take a look at what is included:

♥ **Talkabout:** Most groups need to "break the ice" at the beginning of a session, and here's the question that will do that. It's designed to get people talking around a subject that will be covered in the course of the Bible study.

⬇ **Investigate:** The Bible text for each session is broken up into manageable chunks, with questions that aim to help you understand what the passage is about. **The Leader's Guide** contains **guidance for questions**, and sometimes ⊗ additional "follow-up" questions.

⬇ **Explore more (optional):** These questions will help you connect what you have learned to other parts of the Bible, so you can begin to fit it all together like a jig-saw; or occasionally look at a part of the passage that's not dealt with in detail in the main study.

→ **Apply:** As you go through a Bible study, you'll keep coming across **apply** sections. These are questions to get the group discussing what the Bible teaching means in practice for you and your church. ⊡ **Getting personal** is an opportunity for you to think, plan and pray about the changes that you personally may need to make as a result of what you have learned.

⬆ **Pray:** We want to encourage prayer that is rooted in God's word—in line with his concerns, purposes and promises. So each session ends with an opportunity to review the truths and challenges highlighted by the Bible study, and turn them into prayers of request and thanksgiving.

The **Leader's Guide** and introduction provide historical background information, explanations of the Bible texts for each session, ideas for **optional extra** activities, and guidance on how best to help people uncover the truths of God's word.

Why study Revelation?

Many people find the book of Revelation intimidating, perhaps a bit scary or just plain confusing. But there's no need to be scared—and every reason to be excited.

Imagine looking close up at the details of an impressionist painting. All you can see are strokes of paint and dabs of colour. It's hard to make sense of it. But take a step back, and the picture becomes clear. And what emerges is not just a scene but the mood it evokes. That's how we should approach the book of Revelation. If you lean in too close and look only at the detail—it's all a bit perplexing. But step back, look at the big picture and Revelation not only becomes clearer but it grabs our imaginations.

John is writing to Christians facing the threats and seductions of life in and under the Roman Empire. We need to put ourselves in their shoes and see how Revelation inspires them to remain faithful to Christ, before we apply it to ourselves. Since we are faced with the threat and seductions of the world around us, John wants to recapture our imagination about how God is at work.

Despite everything that is going wrong with our world, God remains in control. And when we see history, our present and our future from heaven's perspective, it will encourage us to trust God and remain faithful to the end.

John does this by presenting to us the visions he receives—visions that take us beyond the chaos of history to see God at work behind the scenes; visions that raise our eyes from this world to the world above, and the world to come. Above all, he shows us a vision of who Jesus Christ is—the ascended reigning Lord, the Lamb who was slain but who now lives for ever, the one who speaks with a voice like the sound of a waterfall, and the one who holds the people of God safe in his hands.

These seven insightful studies will help ordinary Christians see how John's message is just as relevant and applicable to our lives today as it was 2,000 years ago.

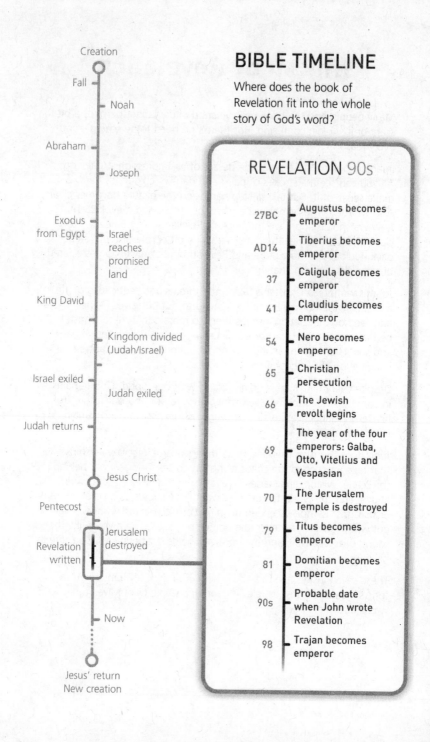

BIBLE TIMELINE

Where does the book of Revelation fit into the whole story of God's word?

Creation
Fall
Noah
Abraham
Joseph
Exodus from Egypt
Israel reaches promised land
King David
Kingdom divided (Judah/Israel)
Israel exiled
Judah exiled
Judah returns
Jesus Christ
Pentecost
Revelation written
Jerusalem destroyed
Now
Jesus' return
New creation

REVELATION 90s

27BC	Augustus becomes emperor
AD14	Tiberius becomes emperor
37	Caligula becomes emperor
41	Claudius becomes emperor
54	Nero becomes emperor
65	Christian persecution
66	The Jewish revolt begins
69	The year of the four emperors: Galba, Otto, Vitellius and Vespasian
70	The Jerusalem Temple is destroyed
79	Titus becomes emperor
81	Domitian becomes emperor
90s	Probable date when John wrote Revelation
98	Trajan becomes emperor

1

Revelation 1

THE LORD WHO REVEALS

⊕ talkabout

1. What are your feelings as you approach these studies in the book of Revelation? If you are feeling nervous or excited, can you explain why?

- From your previous knowledge of this book, how might you summarise its message to a Christian friend, or to someone who is not a Christian?

⊕ investigate

▶ **Read Revelation 1 v 1-11**

2. What is this a revelation of (v 1; see also v 19)?

- What is the five-link chain that has led to you reading it now?

3. According to verse 4, what will be the result of us reading this book? How does this compare with your answer to question 1?

4. How does verse 5 fill out our understanding of what being blessed by God's grace and peace means for those who receive them?

⊡ **explore more**

▶ **Read Revelation 22 v 16-17**

What is the big application of the whole of the book of Revelation?

What should it cause us to do (v 17)?

Sevens and symbols: In this section, we encounter the first example of something peculiar to Revelation and books like Daniel. Apocalyptic literature uses a system of symbols to communicate truths about God powerfully. Here "the seven spirits before his throne" (1 v 4) is simply a description of the Holy Spirit. Seven is the number of perfection or completeness. It is telling us that the Spirit of God is all-present and all-seeing—he is everywhere and sees everything. There is more detail on the meaning of these symbols on page 12.

5. What situation do John and the churches he is writing to face (v 9)?

- Given what we know about the number seven, what is the significance of the churches listed in verse 11?

⊕ investigate

❯ Read Revelation 1 v 12-20

We are not meant to imagine what this figure looks like. Jesus is described with symbols drawn from the Old Testament that tell us something about who he is and what he is doing now.

DICTIONARY

Hades (v 18): the realm of the dead in Greek mythology.

6. Can you decode the symbolic meanings in this description of Jesus? What Old Testament images do they bring to mind?

- Robe:

- Hair (see Daniel 7 v 9):

- Eyes:

- Feet (see Daniel 10 v 6):

- Voice:

- Stars (see Daniel 12 v 3):

- Sword (see Isaiah 11 v 4; Hebrews 4 v 12-13):

- Face (see Exodus 33 v 20):

- *Where* is the figure that John sees? What is the significance of that?

⊡ apply

7. What opposition or pressure do you and your church face today?

• How will this vision of Jesus encourage you to be bold and to persevere in your struggle against these powers?

8. Why is John's response the only appropriate reaction to seeing Jesus as he really is?

9. How is Jesus' response to John so encouraging for him, and for us?

⊡ getting personal

Does your understanding of who Jesus is match up with what was revealed to John?

What emotions do you feel when you come to him in prayer? What emotions should you feel, if you understand who Christ is correctly?

⤓ investigate

10. How might each of the descriptions Jesus gives of himself encourage John and the churches he is writing to as they face hostility and division?

11. What is Jesus' relationship with his beleaguered people (v 20)?

→ apply

12. What is there in your life that will last? What will truly make a difference in eternity?

↑ pray

Spend some time praising the risen Lord Jesus. Use some of the descriptions from the passage, and their meanings, to inform your praises for all that Christ is and has done for us.

Pray for yourselves as individuals and as a group as you read the Father's revelation to you. Pray that you would read it rightly, and understand how it comforts, warns and encourages us.

Pray that you would become faithful witnesses to the grace and peace to be found in Jesus. Ask the Lord to help you find and make opportunities to share Jesus with others as you read this book together.

Symbols in Revelation

The word translated "made … known" in 1 v 1 is literally "signified". Revelation is written in the language of "Sign". In Daniel 2 King Nebuchadnezzar dreams of a statue that is crushed by a stone that becomes a mountain. Daniel makes known this mystery to the king. The four parts of the statue are four great kingdoms, and the stone is God's kingdom. The dream is clearly not to be taken literally. Its components are all symbols that signify something that takes place in history. The same is true of the book of Revelation. It doesn't describe events that will literally take place at some point in the future. It's written in symbols because its aim is not merely to convey information but to capture our imagination. Here is a brief guide to the meaning of some of them. For further help, refer to *Revelation for You*.

Seven: completeness or perfection (perhaps from the seven days of creation)

Six: incompleteness or imperfection (one less than the completeness symbolised by seven)

Seven spirits or sevenfold Spirit: the ever-present Spirit of God (seven signifies his complete or perfect presence)

Four: completeness, especially geographic completeness (the four corners of the earth)

Horn: strength

Eyes: sight or wisdom (insight)

Sea: the forces of chaos (so a crystal sea represents complete control over the forces of chaos)

Living creatures: power or imperial powers

White robes: God's declaration of the wearer's purity, righteousness and vindication, and therefore also the right to be in God's presence

Earthquakes: Earth-shattering events

1,000: many

12: completeness for God's people (from the twelve patriarchs of the Old Testament and twelve apostles of the New Testament)

144,000: 12 x 12 x 1000 = completeness x many = all God's many people

Rainbow: covenant faithfulness and mercy (from Noah's rainbow)

Virginity: faithfulness to God (ready for the marriage of the Lamb)

Adultery: unfaithfulness to God

Trumpets: warnings of judgment, victory or battle

2 Revelation 2 – 3
SEVEN DANGERS FACING YOUR CHURCH

The story so far

John has received a revelation from God which aims to encourage Christians to remain faithful witnesses in a culture that is hostile to Christian beliefs. It starts with a compelling picture of the power of the risen Christ.

⊕ talkabout

1. What is the most significant letter (or email or text) you have ever received? Describe how you felt when you read it and how you reacted afterwards.

2. "What is the biggest problem with the church?" How might people in the street answer that question in general? How might you answer it for the church in general?

   • How would you answer it for your own church?

⊥ investigate

These seven messages are rooted in the specific challenges faced by each congregation. But they are also a word for every church throughout time, and today. They are not just what the Spirit spoke to a church then. They are what the Spirit says to the churches now.

> ▶ **Choose one or more of these messages to read: Ephesus, 2 v 1-7; Pergamum, 2 v 12-17; Thyatira, 2 v 18-28; Sardis, 3 v 1-6; Philadelphia, 3 v 7-13; Laodicea, 3 v 14-22.**

Each letter follows a pattern, which starts with one of the elements of the description of Christ in 1 v 12-16. It is this Jesus who walks among his people, and who speaks words of encouragement and rebuke to them.

3. Fill in the table for at least two of the churches.

Church		
Who is speaking?		
What does he commend?		
What is his complaint?		
What is his command?		
What promise is given?		

4. What do you think it might have been like to be part of the church you have chosen to think about? What would have been great? What would have been disquieting? What would have been bad?

5. How is the description of Jesus particularly relevant to the situation this church faced?

6. How do you think individual church members might have reacted to the rebuke and the challenge presented to them?
How might the church as a whole have responded?

⊟ **apply**

7. Where do you see the problem you have been thinking about in churches today around the world?

8. What about your own church? What would Jesus' challenge to your own church look like today? What would he call you to repent of as a church?

⊡ getting personal

It is easy to point the finger elsewhere: to other churches and their failings. To other members of our own congregation who we think might be "letting the side down". How are you complicit in your church's failings? What is Jesus calling you to repent of? How are you responding to that call?

⊡ explore more

optional

▶ **Read Revelation 2 v 8-11**

What's different about this message to most of the others?

What three pressures do these Christians face (v 9-10)?

What three reassurances does the Spirit give them?

⊡ investigate

▶ **Skim-read Revelation 2 – 3**

9. What were the different sources of the pressures these churches were under that led to their compromise or failure?

➔ apply

10. Which of these sources of personal, internal or external opposition is your church facing at the moment? Which is the most dangerous?

11. Look at the promises and invitations that Jesus makes to his people at the conclusion of each of the messages. Which of these do you think is particularly pertinent to:

• the church in your country as a whole?

• your church in particular?

⊡ getting personal

Which of these promises do you need to hear and embrace now? What will the challenges be for you in doing that?

⬆ pray

Despite all the compromise, lack of love and failure of our churches, Jesus still holds us in his hands. We belong to him and are precious to him.

Give thanks that Jesus loves us so much that he will not abandon us, and that he rebukes and encourages us to be faithful and to grow.

Pray for those churches, like Smyrna, that are facing extreme hostility and persecution. Pray that they would know the Lord's comfort, presence and blessing.

And pray for your own church—asking the Lord to grant you the ability to repent, both as individuals and as a whole, and to listen to what the Spirit is saying to you.

3 Revelation 4 – 5
A HIGHER THRONE

The story so far

John's revelation shows how Jesus is more powerful than the hostile culture we live in. All our problems, deficiencies and struggles as individuals and churches are met by the word and promise of this mighty risen Lord.

⊕ talkabout

1. What are some common views about what heaven will be like among both Christians and non-Christians?

   • What is right and wrong about these ideas, and what do they show about our hopes of the afterlife?

⊕ investigate

After relaying the words of Jesus to churches in real trouble on earth, John is invited to step into heaven to gain an eternal perspective on all the difficulties Christian believers face.

❯ **Read Revelation 4**

> **DICTIONARY**
>
> **Jasper and ruby (v 3):** coloured gemstones.
> **Elders (v 4):** community representatives or leaders.

2. Who and what does John see in this vision of heaven?

• What do the various people and objects in the throneroom represent?

3. What and who is at the centre of heaven?

• What does the reaction of the others present tell us about who this is?

4. What do the two hymns that are sung in this chapter tell us about God?

⤷ apply

5. How would this vision have helped the churches in chapters 2 – 3?

⊡ explore more

> **Read Ezekiel 1 and/or Daniel 7**

What elements are the same as or similar to those in Revelation 4?

How are these ideas extended to the situation John finds himself in?

⊡ getting personal

"Why doesn't God help me?" "What's God up to?" John's vision reminds us that we are not at the centre of the world. This is God's world, not ours. At stake is God's glory, not mine. Everything exists to glorify God. God doesn't exist to serve me or follow my agenda. If you are experiencing suffering, this perspective is both humbling and liberating. You are not in control in your life; God is. And he has the right to order your circumstances as he sees fit. Will you believe that? Will you trust in the God who rules, and give glory to him whatever happens?

⊡ investigate

> **Read Revelation 5**

Chapter 4 is like the scenery of a stage. In chapter 5 the drama begins.

6. What does John see in v 1-4? What do you think this might represent?

DICTIONARY

Scroll (v 1): rolled up parchment.
Seals (v 1): wax that fastens a scroll.
Incense (v 8): substance that gives off a fragrance when burned, used in temple worship.
Slain (v 9): killed.

• Why does John react as he does?

7. How do the descriptions of the Lamb in verses 6-8 build to show us who John is talking about?

8. The song in verses 9-10 explains how the Lamb has become worthy. What did he do and for whom?

• What makes the Lamb different to the rulers and leaders who might be found in an earthly throne room, presidential palace or a parliament?

9. What is the overwhelming response in verses 11-14 to what the Lamb has done?

⮂ apply

10. How might you explain the essence of the Christian message to people from just these two chapters of Revelation?

11. What do verses 9-10 tell us about who the gospel is for, and what our mission is as Christians?

⊡ **getting personal**

It's all about the glory of God and the mission of the Lamb—it's not about you. Is that your perspective? Can you truly sing the songs of Revelation 4 and 5, or are you hesitant to remove your crown and cast it before the One on the throne? Talk to God about your honest answers to those questions.

⊙ **pray**

Ask the One who sits on the throne to help you see the world, your life and your church from heaven's perspective.

Give thanks to the Lamb, who was slain and has purchased you for God with his blood, and made you a kingdom of priests to serve him.

Commit yourself to serving the Lamb, and reigning with him—whatever that might involve.

4 THE CHAOS OF HISTORY

The story so far

God's people struggle to remain faithful to Christ and the gospel mission in a culture that both oppresses them and encourages them to compromise. John's vision shows that God is in control and is the ultimate authority in the universe.

⊕ talkabout

1. What are the biggest, most shocking events in world news that you have ever experienced? How did you feel as you heard of them, or watched them unfold on the news?

⊕ investigate

▶ **Read Revelation 6**

The opening of the seven seals is the first of several cycles of sevens that portray the world's history and its end.

2. The first four seals: What do each of these four horsemen do (v 1-6)? How many people are affected?

> **DICTIONARY**
>
> **Plague (v 8):** a widespread disease.
> **Sovereign (v 10):** in control.

• How does the colour of each horse reflect the activity of its rider?

3. What repeated phrase (v 2, 4 and 8) makes it clear who is in charge?

4. The fifth seal: what is the significance of who we see in verse 9 and where they are?

• What do they pray for (v 10), and what must they wait for (v 11)?

5. The sixth seal: what event is portrayed when the sixth seal is opened (v 12-17)?

• What two reactions are there to this event (v 10, implied, and 15-17)?

6. What is the implied answer to the haunting question in verse 17?

⊕ apply

7. How was this picture of the world under the four horsemen accurate then, and how has it played out throughout history? What about now?

• What should the implications be for us as we witness war, disaster, famine or unrest at home or in other countries?

⊡ getting personal

Do you find God's sovereignty over disaster a difficult truth to embrace? What do you find uncomfortable about it? What do you find comforting in it?

⊡ explore more

Read Revelation 7

John sees the same scene from a different perspective—the four winds are best seen as the equivalent of the four horsemen. But here the focus is on the security of God's people.

How do we know that the number of people "sealed" is symbolic (v 4-8, 9)?

What is the significance of their clothes, and how have they got to a place of safety?

What blessings do God's people enjoy, both now and in eternity?

investigate

The camera angle changes once again. In the sequence of seven trumpets, we see the same scene in close-up focusing on the experience of God's people in a world where the four horsemen ride.

Read Revelation 11 v 1-13

DICTIONARY

Abyss (v 7): realm of evil and darkness.
Sodom (v 8): ancient city that God destroyed in judgment.

8. Who do you think the two witnesses represent (also referred to as olive trees and lampstands, v 4)?

- What power has God given to them? What does this remind you of from the Old Testament?

9. What happens to them, and how do the people react (v 9-10)?

10. What happens next, and how do the people react (v 11-12)?

- Where do the witnesses end up?

11. What happens in response to the miracle of the raising of the witnesses? What is the significance of that?

⊡ **apply**

Chapters 10 – 11 take place in a pause between the sixth and seventh trumpets. The sixth event in each of John's sequences describes the return of Christ and the final judgment. The job of the church today is to faithfully bear the gospel message to everyone as we wait for Christ's return.

12. Who are you fearful of sharing the gospel with? What makes us hesitant?

• What encouragement to persevere with gospel proclamation have you seen in this section of Revelation?

⊡ **getting personal**

In these chapters God's people die and live. Because we're united to Christ, our lives are shaped by his death and resurrection. His death and resurrection are not just the means of our salvation; they're also the pattern for our lives. We die to self and live to God. Whenever you see a lively, living church or people receiving spiritual life, you can be sure that behind the scenes, often unnoticed, someone is working hard, denying themselves and making sacrifices.

In what ways are you dying to yourself to bring life to others?

⊡ pray

Pray for any situations you know where the horsemen ride through the world, or through your own life. Pray that God would have mercy and use people's experience of suffering to lead them to repentance and faith in Christ.

Thank God that those who belong to Jesus have been sealed for eternity. Praise him for the certainty of salvation, forgiveness and our ultimate home with him in heaven.

Ask God to fulfil his purpose of gospel proclamation today, through your church, through missionaries... and through you.

5

Revelation 12 – 16

WHO DO YOU WORSHIP?

The story so far

John has passed on to us his revelation from heaven of the greatness and glory of Jesus. The past, present and future are laid bare by subsequent revelations that show God is in control, and that his people are safe in his care.

⊕ talkabout

1. Do you know anyone who has given up being a Christian? What happened, and what do you think lay behind that decision?

   • When have you been most tempted to give up? What happened, and how did you hang on?

⊥ investigate

Revelation 12 retells the whole of human history as a drama involving three characters: a woman, a child and a dragon.

Remember that apocalyptic literature is full of symbols—things that are to be taken figuratively. And a symbol can stand both for a particular event, person or place and for a more general principle that holds true for more than one event, person or place.

> **Read Revelation 12**

2. Who do the characters in the story represent, and what is the motivation of each? (Hint: There may be more than one answer for the woman.)

3. What does the dragon try to do to the child and the woman's other offspring, and how is he thwarted?

• What incidents in the life of Christ and the church does this remind you of?

4. When does the angelic war in verses 7-9 take place? What do you think it refers to?

• What can Satan no longer do, according to verse 10? Why?

5. What is Satan doing now, according to verses 13-17?

⊙ apply

6. How should Christians therefore think about Satan, the church, and our own discipleship?

optional

⊙ explore more

❯ **Read 1 Kings 19 v 1-8**

How does Revelation 12 allude to this story, and to Israel's 40 years in the wilderness?

What does it show us about God's care for us?

⊙ getting personal

In what ways do you experience the accusations and hostility of Satan in the course of your everyday life?

⊙ investigate

❯ **Read Revelation 13**

7. What do you think the two beasts represent, from their descriptions?

DICTIONARY

Blasphemies (v 5): words and speech that dishonour God.
Slander (v 6): tell lies about.
Image (v 14): statue that people worship.

• What does the first beast do, and how does the world respond to it?

8. What is confusing about the description of the second beast in verse 11?

• How does it secure its following?

9. How do the two beasts combine to oppress people—and God's people in particular?

10. What do you think the significance is of the marking on the forehead or hand (v 16)?

• What, do you think, is the significance of the number 666 (v 18)?

⊡ **explore more**

> ❯ **Read Ephesians 1 v 13-14; 4 v 30**

How does God mark or "seal" those who belong to him? How do we know we are sealed?

⊟ **apply**

11. Where do you see the beasts at work in the world today?

12. In what practical ways can we help each other to resist the hostility and seduction of our world?

⊡ **getting personal**

When and where do you feel the seduction of the culture most keenly? What do you find more exciting or thrilling than Jesus? Where do you feel the threat of exclusion most powerfully?

⊕ pray

If Satan is accusing you, rejoice that Christ's blood is all you need. If you are facing Satan's hostility, ask the Lord for the strength to love him and the gospel more than your life.

Pray for your brothers and sisters in parts of the world where being a faithful witness can lead to physical harm and death.

Pray that you would resist the seduction of the world, and that your church fellowship would be supportive and nurturing of those who feel this pressure most strongly.

6 Revelation 17 – 20
THE JUSTICE OF THE LAMB

The story so far

Jesus reigns in heaven. His people suffer on earth, threatened and seduced by the ruling power of the day. But God is in control in the chaos of history and will return to judge. Christians must remain faithful gospel witnesses as we wait for his coming.

⊕ talkabout

1. Have you ever had to wait a long time for something? How did you feel during that time?

⊥ investigate

> **Read Revelation 17**

2. What clues are there in this hideous description as to what the figures of the beast and the woman represent?

3. What is John's reaction to this vision, and what's the reaction of those who are not saved (v 6, 8)?

• What is your reaction?

4. What is meant by the repeated phrase "once was, now is not, and yet will come..." (v 7, 8)?

5. What becomes of the beast and the woman in the end (v 10-12, 16)?

→ **apply**

6. What do you find most attractive and enjoyable about the modern world we live in?

7. How can you enjoy these blessings without being consumed by them?

⊡ getting personal

How can you remind yourself day by day, moment by moment, that we walk to the beat of a different drum?

⊡ explore more

▶ Read Revelation 18

The orgy of chapter 17 has turned into a wake, as kings, merchants and sea captains, who all grew rich from "Babylon", mourn her destruction.

What is the verdict of heaven (v 4-8)

18 v 4 commands Christians to "come out of her". What do you think this might mean in practice?

⊡ investigate

▶ **Read Revelation 19 v 1-10**

This study began with an invitation from the great prostitute to join her in sexual immorality and get drunk on her wine (17 v 1-2). It ends with a very different invitation.

> **DICTIONARY**
>
> **Hallelujah (v 1):** praise God!

8. What invitation are we given in verse 5?

9. How should Christians respond to seeing both salvation and judgment?

10. What invitation are we given in verse 9? What does this mean?

11. How does verse 10 underline the response we are called to make?

⊕ apply

12. What are the signs that someone has accepted the invitation to the marriage feast of the Lamb?

⊕ pray

Ask God to help you see the world as it really is. To enjoy the good things, but not fall in love with them or be distracted or compromised by them.

Pray that the Lord would have mercy on our lost world, and that we would remain faithful witnesses—whatever our circumstances.

Give thanks that we have been given the gracious invitation to be part of the marriage feast of the Lamb. Use the songs of praise in chapter 19 to express your thanks to God.

⊡ explore more

optional

▶ **Read Revelation 20 v 1-6**

What explanations have you heard about the meaning of the millennium (1,000-year reign, v 4) pictured in these verses?

What response do you think we should make as we read these words?

7 Revelation 21 – 22
THE REIGN OF THE LAMB

The story so far

John has revealed many things to us: the glory of Jesus; the sovereignty of God over all that happens; the wickedness and evil of the world systems under which we live; the need to remain faithful to Jesus and our task of world mission; and the ultimate judgment of the world when Jesus returns.

⊕ talkabout

1. What are you most looking forward to in eternity?

⊕ investigate

> **Read Revelation 21 v 1 – 22 v 5**

2. What is new, and what has passed away (v 1-4)?

DICTIONARY

Consigned (v 8): put.
Measuring rod (v 15): a measurement ruler.
Book of life (v 27): a book with the names of people who are saved.
Yielding (22 v 2): giving.

3. What will be at the heart of our experience of eternity (v 5-9)?

• What is the significance of each element of the description of the new Jerusalem?

4. What is not present in the new Jerusalem (v 22-27), and what is the significance of each thing mentioned that will be absent?

• What is the significance of verse 26?

5. What is the conclusion to the vision in verse 6?

• What do you think the fulfilment of this promise will be like?

⊖ apply

6. What part of John's vision captures your imagination or speaks to your current challenges?

- How can this vision of eternity help us persevere when things are hard for us?

7. How do people come to be in the new creation (v 27), and what does that encourage us to keep doing?

⊡ getting personal

Are you confident that your name is written in the book of life? What makes you certain of that, and therefore confident that you will enjoy eternity with Christ?

⊡ explore more

> **Read Romans 8 v 18-23 and 2 Peter 3 v 10-13**

Will creation be renewed or replaced?

optional

⊕ investigate

▶ Read Revelation 22 v 6-21

8. What phrase is repeated in verses 7 and 12? How could this have been true when John wrote Revelation 2,000 years ago?

9. What are we to think about the teaching in Revelation, and what are we to do with it (v 6-16)?

10. What final appeal does John want to impress on us (v 17)?

⊖ apply

One helpful way to summarise the message of Revelation is to think about the contrast between the two women: Babylon the Prostitute (chapter 17) and Jerusalem the Bride (chapter 21). The first is destined for destruction; the second is destined for glory.

11. Are you more at home in Babylon the Prostitute or Jerusalem the Bride? What are the signs that would show you which is true for you?

12. How has God spoken to you through the words of Revelation? What specific steps are you going to take in response?

⊡ getting personal

Do you want Christ to come soon, as he promises to do in 22 v 20? Do you pray, "Come, Lord Jesus" as John does? What prevents you from being excited by and hungry for the return of Christ?

↑ pray

Give praise to God for the new creation that you will be part of if you are in Christ. Bring before him the things that make you cry or grieve, or give you pain. Be grateful together that these will all be taken away in God's new creation.

Pray the words of 22 v 20. Ask that Christ would come soon.

Thank God for all he has taught you from your study in Revelation. Be specific about what you have learned.

Leader's Guide to Revelation

INTRODUCTION

Leading a Bible study can be a bit like herding cats—everyone has a different idea of what the passage could be about, and a different line of enquiry that they want to pursue. But a good group leader is more than someone who just referees this kind of discussion. You will want to:

- correctly understand and handle the Bible passage. But also...

- encourage and train the people in your group to do this for themselves. Don't fall into the trap of spoon-feeding people by simply passing on the information in the Leader's Guide. Then...

- make sure that no Bible study is finished without everyone knowing how the passage is relevant for them. What changes do you all need to make in the light of the things you have been learning? And finally...

- encourage the group to turn all that has been learned and discussed into prayer.

Your Bible-study group is unique, and you are likely to know better than anyone the capabilities, backgrounds and circumstances of the people you are leading. That's why we've designed these guides with a number of optional features. If they're a quiet bunch, you might want to spend longer on *talkabout*. If your time is limited, you can choose to skip *explore more*, or get people to look at these questions at home. Can't get enough of Bible study? Well, some studies have optional extra homework projects. As leader, you can adapt and select the material to the needs of your particular group.

So what's in the Leader's Guide? The main thing that this Leader's Guide will help you to do is to understand the major teaching points in the passage you are studying, and how to apply them. As well as guidance for the questions, the Leader's Guide for each session contains the following important sections:

THE BIG IDEA

One or two key sentences will give you the main point of the session. This is what you should be aiming to have fixed in people's minds as they leave the Bible study. And it's the point you need to head back toward when the discussion goes off at a tangent.

SUMMARY

An overview of the passage, including plenty of useful historical background information.

OPTIONAL EXTRA

Usually this is an introductory activity that ties in with the main theme of the Bible study, and is designed to "break the ice" at the beginning of a session. Or it may be a "homework project" that people can tackle during the week.

So let's take a look at the various different features of a Good Book Guide:

⊕ talkabout

Each session kicks off with a discussion question, based on the group's opinions or experiences. It's designed to get people talking and thinking in a general way about the main subject of the Bible study.

⊕ investigate

The first thing you and your group need to know is what the Bible passage is about, which is the purpose of these questions. But watch out—people may come up with answers based on their experiences or teaching they have heard in the past, without referring to the passage at all. It's amazing how often we can get through a Bible study without actually looking at the Bible! If you're stuck for an answer, the Leader's Guide contains guidance for questions. These are the answers to direct your group to. This information isn't meant to be read out to people—ideally, you want them to discover these answers from the Bible for themselves. Sometimes there are optional follow-up questions (see ⊗ in guidance for questions) to help you help your group get to the answer.

⊡ explore more

These questions generally point people to other relevant parts of the Bible. They are useful for helping your group to see how the passage fits into the "big picture" of the whole Bible. These sections are OPTIONAL—only use them if you have time. Remember that it's better to finish in good time having really grasped one big thing from the passage, than to try and cram everything in.

⊖ apply

We want to encourage you to spend more time working at application—too often, it is simply tacked on at the end. In the Good Book Guides, apply sections are mixed in with the investigate sections of the study. We hope that people will realise that application is not just an optional extra, but rather, the whole purpose of studying the

Bible. We do Bible study so that our lives can be changed by what we hear from God's word. If you skip the application, the Bible study hasn't achieved its purpose.

These questions draw out practical lessons that we can all learn from the Bible passage. You can review what has been learned so far, and think about practical differences that this should make in our churches and our lives. The group gets the opportunity to talk about what they personally have learned.

⊡ getting personal

These can be done at home, but it is well worth allowing a few moments of quiet reflection during the study for each person to think and pray about specific changes they need to make in their own lives. Why not have a time for reporting back at the beginning of the following session, so that everyone can be encouraged and challenged by one another to make application a priority?

⬆ pray

In Acts 4 v 25-30 the first Christians quoted Psalm 2 as they prayed in response to the persecution of the apostles by the Jewish religious leaders. Today however, it's not as common for Christians to base prayers on the truths of God's word as it once was. As a result, our prayers tend to be weak, superficial and self-centred rather than bold, visionary and God-centred.

The prayer section is based on what has been learned from the Bible passage. How different our prayer times would be if we were genuinely responding to what God has said to us through his word.

1 Revelation 1
THE LORD WHO REVEALS

THE BIG IDEA
God the Father, through Jesus reveals the truth about the past, present and the future for his beleaguered people. The biggest thing we need to see is who Jesus really is now.

SUMMARY
Revelation is a form of literature called "apocalyptic", and it is unfamiliar to modern readers, although John's first readers would have understood the form. It portrays past, current and future events, characters, countries and people using vivid symbolism and imagery. It can sometimes feel like being in the middle of a weird dream, where things don't make logical sense and the pictures shift around from one section to another. This has led to this book of the Bible becoming a happy hunting ground for bizarre theories and strange ideas. And so it is not surprising that many believers are a little fearful of what a study of Revelation might involve. Your job as a leader will be, first of all, to reassure your group. Revelation does, indeed deal with the past, the present and the future. But rather than present a precise roadmap to the end to the world, these notes will try to help your group see the bigger purpose in God giving us this letter.

The overall themes of Revelation are simple, encouraging and vital for anyone who, like the first readers, were struggling to remain faithful to Christ in their idolatrous culture. The Roman Empire pushed them towards a conformity and loyalty that were impossible for them to hold together with faith in Christ. And when they refused to conform,

it oppressed them, in both subtle and more brutal and obvious ways.

John's revelation comes to him on the island of Patmos, where he is in exile for remaining faithful to Christ. Although in chapter 1, we are first told that Revelation is about the future (v 1), it is also about the here and now (v 19). And the biggest thing that is revealed to us is that Jesus Christ is the majestic Lord over everything. The symbol-laden description of Jesus stands over everything that follows in this book. He is the one we must worship and fall down before—not angels, and certainly not Rome, or any other culture we happen to live in.

OPTIONAL EXTRA
Play a game of "Startling Revelation". Get the group to bring baby pictures of themselves, or each write on a piece of paper something amazing or unusual that they can do, have done, or has happened to them. The group then has to guess who, and give their reasons, before the startling revelation is made.

GUIDANCE FOR QUESTIONS
Note: These studies cover a lot of ground and a lot of complex ideas. It may be that you want to take it more slowly than seven sessions, depending on what your group can cope with. As we will see, the ideas and applications in Revelation are actually not that complex, but the language and shape of the writing can be quite confusing to people unfamiliar with apocalyptic writing.

1. What are your feelings as you approach these studies in the book of

Revelation? If you are feeling nervous or excited, can you explain why? This question and the one that follows provide a good opportunity to get out into the open how people may be feeling about this book. They may be:

• *overly afraid.* They have heard it is complicated and that Christians disagree (and even fight) over how to interpret and understand it.

• *overly enthusiastic.* Treating it as an area of specialist knowledge, and perhaps seeing things in it that are not helpful.

• *dismissive.* Because it focuses on heaven, hell, judgment and other difficult doctrines for our age and culture, some of your group may think it is not relevant for today.

• **From your previous knowledge of this book, how might you summarise its message to a Christian friend, or to someone who is not a Christian?** Your group's answers to this question will help you understand, as a leader where your group members lack knowledge, understanding or confidence in the message of Revelation.

2. What is this a revelation of (v 1, see also v 19)? There are indeed some strange parts of this book that we find difficult to understand in our day and age. But we should not let that confuse us as to the fundamentals. This is a message from our Lord Jesus, through his servant John (via an angelic messenger), to each one of us who belongs to Christ, both back then when it was written and to us today. This revelation is not only about the *future*, but it is also about *the here and now* (v 19); That is, it speaks about the present as well as the future. And the revelation it contains about our future impacts deeply on how we think and the choices we make now. But above

all, it is a revelation of *who Jesus really is.* This is the focus of this first study: not the future or the present, but the one who is Lord of both the present and the future.

• **What is the five-link chain that has led to you reading it now?** God the Father has given the revelation to Jesus, his Son. Jesus gave it to angels (= messengers) to give to John. John wrote it down for us to read.

3. According to verse 4, what will be the result of us reading this book? How does this compare with your answer to question 1? We will be blessed by God as we read aloud the words of Revelation. We will be blessed by God if we hear these words and keep them. God has promised to bless you during these studies in Revelation—as you read the book together and listen to the message—so long as you keep (= obey, live out) the words. This also helps us to sift out wrong interpretations of Revelation. If someone's interpretation of Revelation doesn't bless their hearers, then something is wrong. The blessings we receive are both grace and peace.

4. How does verse 5 fill out our understanding of what being blessed by God's grace and peace mean for those who receive them? God the Father is the beginning and the end, the almighty one; and he has made Jesus "the ruler of the kings of the earth" (v 5). Despite all the evidence to the contrary, John's readers have backed the winning side.

EXPLORE MORE
Read Revelation 22 v 16-17. What is the big application of the whole of the book of Revelation? What should it cause us to do (v 17)? The Holy Spirit is making his invitation to us through this book to

"come". Come to Jesus to receive the free gift of the water of life. It's a call that the church (the bride) picks up and repeats. This book is meant to result in us renewing and amplifying our appeal to the world to come to Christ, who gives freely to the spiritually thirsty. If you are fearful of what Revelation says, or if suspicious of what might come out of these studies, then relax. What we are working towards is an understanding of this Revelation that will thrill your heart with a fresh appreciation of our Lord and Saviour, Jesus Christ, and fire your soul to reach out to others with the life-saving gospel.

5. What situation do John and the churches he is writing to face (v 9)? John is writing to churches that are suffering, and he writes as a fellow sufferer for he is in exile on Patmos, an island off the coast of Greece.

- **Given what we know about the number seven, what is the significance of the churches listed in verse 11?** Although these particular churches are named, the "seven" suggests that they are meant to represent the whole of the church. This is not a word for merely a few specific people and places back then. This is a word for all of us for all time. The mighty empire of Rome offered its citizens "peace": a freedom from warfare and a legal system that protected their rights. It did not do quite so well on "grace" however. If you opposed the might of Rome, or made it clear that your first allegiance was not to Rome and its emperor, you were in danger of being judged and rejected. This is exactly the situation John's readers find themselves in. Loyalty and devotion to Christ as King meant opposition to Rome. This is the theme that underlies much of the book of Revelation.

6. Can you decode the symbolic meanings in this description of Jesus? What Old Testament images do they bring to mind? This passage is filled with allusions to the Old Testament. The "someone like a son of man" is straight out of Daniel 7, and the other symbols are designed to impress upon us his authority, his ability to judge, his purity, his glory, his wisdom and his willingness to fight on behalf of his people.

- **Where is the figure that John sees? What is the significance of that?** Jesus stands, not separate and distant from the beleaguered churches of ancient Rome, but "among the lampstands". He is right there with them as they face the tension and pressure of living in a hostile, aggressive world.

7. APPLY: What opposition or pressure do you and your church face today? Get the group to see that it is not just active persecution that we struggle with, but also our seduction by a system and a culture that seems to offer us wealth, acceptance, status and protection. The physical dangers are very real in some countries. But we must not overplay the hostile opposition we face in western countries. Our danger is being seduced into living low-grade Christian lives as we compromise with the culture.

- **How will this vision of Jesus encourage you to be bold and to persevere in your struggle against these powers?** Be very practical about connecting aspects of Jesus' Lordship and power with specific threats. E.g. if Jesus holds the keys to death and Hades, we should not fear death; if he is the giver of life, we should not believe anyone else who claims that what they offer is more fulfilling and life giving than Christ.

8. APPLY: Why is John's response the only appropriate reaction to seeing Jesus as he really is? When we see Jesus in all his glory, our only reaction is to fall down and worship him, in love and gratitude if we have been forgiven, or in dread fear if we have not. The startling vision of the glory and power of Jesus that John receives is totally overwhelming. This is the same feeling experienced by, for example, Isaiah in the temple (Isaiah 6 v 5) or Peter in the Gospels (Luke 5 v 8).

9. APPLY: How is Jesus' response to John so encouraging for him, and for us? The might of the Roman Empire is lined up against the church, and the message of Jesus is, "Do not be afraid". But the striking thing is this: John has not fallen before the Roman Empire. It's not Rome that makes him afraid. It is the risen Jesus. When you see Jesus as who he really is, you fall at his feet. It knocks you out! It's not Rome or its modern equivalents that we need to fear. Rome is not the mighty One. It's Jesus.

10. How might each of the descriptions Jesus gives of himself encourage John and the churches he is writing to as they face hostility and division? Because he died and rose again, the Lord Jesus Christ now holds the keys of death and Hades (v 18). Keys are a symbol of authority. A key-holder has control over a building. Jesus has authority over death. He can unlock death and let you out. The message is clear: the state may lock you up or even kill you; but Jesus holds the keys that matter. Imprisonment and death should hold no fear for those who belong to Jesus. Whatever we endure for him in this life will be worth it because Jesus himself is the promise of eternal life.

11. What is Jesus' relationship with his beleaguered people (v 20)? We may also be distressed when we see whole churches that are struggling with threats from without, or with divisions and false teaching from within. Jesus holds these precious stars in his hand. His angels move among the lampstands to guard and guide. We can be sure we are not abandoned, even when things seem at their worst.

12. APPLY: What is there in your life that will last? What will make a difference in eternity? The people around us who live for themselves or for pleasure are doing the sensible thing, given their belief that death is the end. But we believe in life after death—because Jesus rose from the dead. We believe in the living One, who holds the keys of death and Hades. And this gives meaning and purpose to our lives. It gives us a life that will not be in vain—a life that will count for all eternity.

2 Revelation 2 – 3
SEVEN DANGERS FACING YOUR CHURCH

THE BIG IDEA
Jesus cares for the church—his people—and urges them to remain faithful in the face of the hostility and seduction of the culture.

SUMMARY
Most New Testament letters follow a pattern of first deepening our understanding of who God is and what he has done for us in the gospel. Only then are these truths applied to how we live, often in the second half of an epistle. Right belief before right action: orthodoxy before orthopraxy. In Revelation this is reversed. After a brief introduction to the letter, and the powerful revelation of the powerful Lord Jesus in chapter 1, John immediately goes on to apply what being faithful followers of Christ and faithful congregations of believers means in chapters 2 and 3.

Although these messages were written to specific churches in Asia Minor (today's Turkey), there is a universality about the encouragements, rebukes,and appeals that Jesus makes to these seven congregations. To each church he says, "Whoever has ears, let them hear what the Spirit says to the churches". These seven messages are rooted in the specific challenges faced by each congregation. But they are also a word for every church today. They are not just what the Spirit spoke to a church. They are what the Spirit says to all churches. They are what the Spirit is saying in our day to the churches of our day.

But some of these churches were also compromised. They were being pulled away from following Christ by their culture. They did not face hostility from the outside because, if truth be told, they were not so very different from the world around them.

Jesus brings a message of comfort and hope to those who are suffering for their faith. He brings a wake-up call to those who are compromised. He speaks in love of the love that really matters. Not love for the world, but a deep love for Jesus—and a desire to please him by the way we live. He tells us what is truly important. He offers great resources to those who remain faithful. He promises great rewards to those who overcome.

The seven messages in Revelation 2 – 3 have features common to most of them:
• a reminder of who speaks to the church
• a commendation
• a complaint
• a command
• a call to listen to the Spirit
• a promise to those who overcome
People often call them "letters", but Revelation describes them as "words" or "messages". They are not separate letters, but part of the book of Revelation as a whole. They each begin with a reminder of John's vision of the risen Christ in 1 v 12-16. And they each end with a promise that points forward to some aspect of John's vision in the rest of the book. Some of John's readers were facing persecution (1 v 9; 2 v 9, 13). But persecution was not widespread or systematic when Revelation was most likely to have been written (in

the last decade of the first century). In part, John's vision was preparing Christians for what might come. But it was also concerned about Christians who were compromising with the culture. These are "words" we need to hear today.

Note to leaders: There is way too much content here for a fruitful discussion that covers each of the seven churches spoken to. Also, the danger to avoid is to allow the session to become one where other churches and Christians are criticised for having the weaknesses or failures of one of the examples in these chapters. As a leader, you need to help your group focus on themselves and your own church. This may well prove to be an uncomfortable exercise. Avoid criticising leaders and the hierarchy of the church, and focus on what Jesus is saying to you, and on how you can be both encouraged and challenged to repent and be a faithful witness.

Here are some ideas of how you might fruitfully use your time to be more focussed.

1. After the general introductory questions, choose just one of the churches to focus on. Choose the section you focus on carefully and prayerfully as the one that you believe most fits your own situation as a fellowship.

2. If you have a lot of group members, split the group up individually or into pairs to look at one church each and fill in the table. As you discuss the application questions that follow, go to each of them to share how they would apply the "word" they looked at to your own situation.

3. As above, but choose two or three churches to look at that you think have a particular bearing on your own situation.

OPTIONAL EXTRA

At the start: Read old letter you have received, or one you have inherited from parents. Get people to guess its significance. Use this to lead into Question 1. Or Google "famous letters" and find some great letters written in history by famous people. Read out a few snippets, and ask who they were from and who they were writing to. E.g. *"A few days ago I thought I loved you; but since I last saw you I feel I love you a thousand times more. All the time I have known you, I adore you more each day … I beg you, let me see some of your faults: be less beautiful, less graceful, less kind, less good…"*
(Napoleon Bonaparte to Josephine, 1790s).
"My blind eyes are desperately waiting for the sight of you. You don't realise of course, E.B., how fascinatingly beautiful you have always been, and how strangely you have acquired an added and special and dangerous loveliness."
(Richard Burton to Elizabeth Taylor, 1964).
"Consider well, my mistress, that absence from you grieves me sorely, hoping that it is not your will that it should be so; but if I knew for certain that you voluntarily desired it, I could do no other than mourn my ill-fortune, and by degrees abate my great folly. And so, for lack of time, I make an end of this rude letter, beseeching you to give credence to this bearer in all that he will tell you from me."Written by the hand of your entire Servant, H.R.
(Henry VIII to Anne Boleyn).
At the end: Get hold of *Seven Dangers Facing Your Church* by Juan Sanchez, and use it as a "book group" book for your group to discuss over the following weeks.

GUIDANCE FOR QUESTIONS
1. What is the most significant letter (or email or text) you have ever received?

Describe how you felt when you read it and how you reacted afterwards. It might be an exam result letter, or one informing you of a death, or being dumped by text. Prepare a couple of things including something light and something serious.

2. "What is the biggest problem with the church?" How might people in the street answer that question in general? How might you answer it for the church in general? Outdated, irrelevant, boring, hypocritical. Take your pick. It is worth getting the group to reflect on how others see us, before we take a look at how God sees us.

- **How would you answer it for your own church?** Make sure that this question does not spark a complaining session. Move on quickly to how God sees the problems in our congregations.

3. Fill in the table for at least two of the churches. There may be discussion around the precise meaning of some of the challenges and promises. Refer to *Revelation For You* pages 36-47 for more detailed comment on these.

4. What do you think it might have been like to be part of the church you have chosen to think about? What would have been great? What would have been disquieting? What would have been bad? Try to get the group to see how these might have been exciting or privileged churches to belong to, and yet there were disturbing undercurrents.

5. How is the description of Jesus particularly relevant to the situation this church faced? Look back to the last study to see the meaning of the images applied to Jesus there.

6. How do you think individual church members might have reacted to the rebuke and the challenge presented to them? How might the church as a whole have responded? Again, people are free to use their imagination here. Answers must take account of pride and lack of self-awareness, as people are rebuked for things they are unaware of or have grown accustomed to; but also of gratitude, relief and comfort for things that were a worrying concern for them.

7. APPLY: Where do you see the problem you have been thinking about in churches today around the world? Allow the group to discuss issues relating to active persecution in various parts of the world, and internal struggles with false teaching. But don't let the group forget that seduction by the world and lovelessness are also a part of the landscape here. The warnings of these two chapters cover the silent sickness and slow demise of churches through simply falling in love with the world, and growing cold in their love for Jesus.

8. APPLY: What about your own church? What would Jesus' challenge to your own church look like today? What would he call you to repent of as a church? Make sure that this discussion does not descend into a criticism of church leaders, or people assume that the problem is with others, not themselves. Encourage people to use the pronouns "we" and "us" when talking about your congregation—not "you" and "them". It might be a good place to pause and pray specifically for your own church congregation and leaders. If people feel strongly about something relating to this, you could, perhaps, write a joint letter to your church leaders about the issue, in a spirit of humility and repentance.

EXPLORE MORE

Read Revelation 2 v 8-11. What's different about this message to most of the others? Jesus has nothing to condemn the church at Smyrna for.

What three pressures do these Christians face (v 9-10)? Unlike five of the other messages, there is no word of complaint—just pastoral encouragement for struggling Christians. They face the pressures of poverty (v 9), slander (v 9) and persecution (v 10). The source of persecution is the Jewish community (v 9).

What three reassurances does the Spirit give them? 1. Christ's presence: "I know your afflictions" (v 9). 2. God's control: The Christians are persecuted by Satan (v 10). There is a battle between God and Satan (chapter 12), but God is in control. "Ten" in 2 v.10 symbolises fulness. 3. Eternal reward: Our hope is based on the fact that Jesus is "the First and the Last, who died and came to life again" (v 8). The crown in verse 10 probably refers to the royal crown: the reward to faithful disciples, who will rule with Christ.

9. What were the different sources of the pressures these churches were under that led to their compromise or failure?
Personal: A desire for comfort, an easy life, and a sense of pride about what we have all feature in some of these churches. *Internal:* False teaching within the church; a culture of luke warmness; immorality that is tolerated. *External:* Direct persecution; a culture of hostility.

10. APPLY: Which of these sources of personal, internal or external opposition is your church facing at the moment? Which is the most dangerous? For most Christians in the developed world, it is the personal desire for comfort and an easy life which is most dangerous. But false teaching is also an ever present danger. In some ways, external pressure in the form of persecution can be an enormous help to people, as it clarifies the issues about what is important, and encourages us to more devoted discipleship that we struggle to maintain in times of relative ease.

11. APPLY: Look at the promises and invitations that Jesus makes to his people at the conclusion of each of the messages. Which of these do you think is particularly pertinent to:
• **the church in your country as a whole.**
• **your church in particular?**
Make a note of what people say here, and use the points in your prayer time together.

3 Revelation 4 – 5
A HIGHER THRONE

THE BIG IDEA

God—Father, Son and Holy Spirit—is on the throne and rules everything. We are tempted to think that God is not in control, or that we are the centre of things.

SUMMARY

In the New Testament, we often have theology first and application second. In Revelation it's the other way around. The letters to the churches were application and now we get the big picture. As you read this astonishing chapter, try to get your group to build a picture in their minds of what the scene looked like to John.

In the book of Revelation, John is opening our eyes to the unseen world, just as Elisha prayed for his servant in 2 Kings 6 v 14-17. We still see the "Aramean army" around us. But we're given a vision of "chariots of fire". We still see history from the perspective of the earth. But now we can also see it from the perspective of heaven. Imagine you are in a dark room with one chink of light. All around are dark, shadowy shapes. Then you move so that your eyes are directly in the beam of light. In that moment everything changes. Suddenly you see beyond the dark room across millions of miles to the sun, burning with fierce splendour. The brilliance of the light makes the room around you almost invisible. That's the movement John is inviting us to make. We see darkness and shadows all around us. We also recognise that light is breaking through. Occasionally we see flecks transfigured into something like stardust. But John is inviting us to move into the full beam of light and have our vision transformed so that light consumes

darkness and reality replaces shadows. Be prepared for your eyes to hurt.

There are many defective views of what heaven will be like. It is important to note that any image or picture of eternity will be insufficient—we do not have the language to describe it, and so we are given pictures filled with symbols that hint at how immense and glorious it is. The point to note is that it is not about harps, mansions or any of the other physical trappings. It is fundamentally about God and being close to him. The throne is in the centre, and everything revolves around that. And worship and praise of God is the constant theme that underlies this picture. The sense we get from chapter 4 is that God is great and glorious, and that we are small and blessed—and therefore joyful. In chapter 5 we are introduced to a mysterious scroll, a symbol of God's good plan of salvation for a universe that is hostile to him and appears out of control. John weeps that the scroll cannot be opened—but then heaven rejoices because the Lamb, who is alive and standing but looks as though it has been slain (5 v 6), is considered worthy to open the scroll. This is, of course, a picture of Jesus.

Through his life, death and resurrection, the Lord Jesus Christ is worthy to open, or enact, the scroll of God's salvation plan for the world. The end point of our reading these chapters will be to join in heaven's praise to the greatness and glory of God, and to worship the Lamb for what he has done. This vision will enable us to remain wise about what is truly important, and to persevere as we struggle to remain faithful.

OPTIONAL EXTRA

There are many popular songs that talk about heaven, often with wrong thinking in them. Have some music about heaven playing in the background as people arrive. As you listen to the lyrics, discuss what the view of heaven is, and what is deficient about it.

Alternatively, pass around some coins or banknotes from different countries. Talk about the way that animals are symbols of countries and regimes: on British coins you find a lion; on American coins an eagle; France a cockerel; China, a dragon; Russia a bear, etc. Ask: Why do we use these representations—what are they meant to convey?

GUIDANCE FOR QUESTIONS

1. What are some common views about what heaven will be like among both Christians and non-Christians? Some think we will be without bodies and just "spiritual"—floating on clouds with harps, dressed in nighties. Others paint a vision of heaven that is an extension of church: endless hymn singing. Others believe in an extended version of what we consider to be joyful on earth—a fulfilment of our personal desires: an endless party; flowing wine; in the case of some Muslim visions of heaven, enjoying endless sexual pleasure. Others, of course, think there is no afterlife, but just oblivion.

• **What is right and wrong about these ideas, and what do they show about our hopes of the afterlife?** These views of the afterlife miss out the main feature of biblical descriptions of eternity—relationship: with each other and with God. They are also often about self-justification or an amplification of the pleasures of this life, and very

individual—not about the glory of God and the blessing of living in a redeemed community.

2. Who and what does John see in this vision of heaven? John sees someone seated on a throne, surrounded by 24 elders on other thrones. He sees seven burning lamps in front of the throne, and four living creatures full of eyes.

• **What do the various people and objects in the throneroom represent?** The person on the throne: God the Father. Seven torches: the Holy Spirit (7 = perfection). 24 elders: a symbol of both old and new covenants from the 12 tribes of Israel and the 12 apostles—they most likely represent the totality of God's people throughout history. The four beasts are drawn from Ezekiel's vision of God's throne (Ezekiel 1), together with the six wings and song of the seraphs in Isaiah 6:2-3; they represent the praise of all animate creation. **Note:** The vision also reflects the way idolatrous powers use animal symbols of strength and aggression to represent themselves.

3. What and who is at the centre of heaven? A throne, with God upon it. God is at the centre and is supremely powerful.

• **What does the reaction of the others present tell us about who this is?** They worship and adore him, and give all their glory to him. Even the creatures, who represent the idolatrous powers of the day, live in service to him, not themselves. They don't proclaim the glory of their earthly kingdoms. They proclaim the power of heaven's King. The hymns of Revelation make explicit the point being made symbolically by the imagery.

4. What do the two hymns that are sung in this chapter tell us about God? Note the contrast with earthly kingdoms. God is holy. God always was, is present now, and always will be. God is the creator of all things. He is worthy to receive glory and honour and power (implication: the kingdom's of this world are not). Our very existence depends on God.

5. APPLY: How would this have vision helped the churches in chapters 2 – 3? They were either struggling or compromised or both. Those churches needed a vision of God's reign if they were to endure their suffering or end their compromise. Chapter 4 is full of political imagery—thrones, crowns, imperial animals (remember that, as far as the empire was concerned, John was a political prisoner). But it's all subservient to God. The twenty-four elders get down from their thrones and take off their crowns to bow before the throne of God. Twice God is described as "him who lives for ever and ever" (v 9-10). This is Jesus' response to the claims of "eternal Rome". Rome appeared to rule all the known world, but God rules in heaven.

EXPLORE MORE
Read Ezekiel 1 and/or Daniel 7. What elements are the same as or similar to those in Revelation 4? The vision of Revelation 4 is full of echoes of the visions of Ezekiel 1 and Daniel 7. These visions both came in Babylon just as John's vision came in the symbolic 'Babylon' of the Roman empire. Ezekiel sees God on a moving throne with all-seeing eyes. Even in Babylon, in the stronghold of empire, God is reigning. Daniel also has a vision of empires: four successive empires which are superseded by another empire whose dominion will never end (Daniel 7). The Ancient of Days gives all

authority to the people of God represented by the son of man.

How are these ideas extended to the situation John finds himself in? The churches to which John wrote saw Roman imperial rule with all its splendour and imagery. It was constantly in their sight-line. They were tempted to compromise or give up. God appears to be absent from history and others appear to be lords. But John sees God on the throne and his reign radically relativises other rulers.

6. What does John see in v 1-4? What do you think this might represent? John sees a scroll with seven seals in the right hand of the one on the throne (v 1). What it contains we are not told. Perhaps it is God's plan for the restoration of the world. It is important to note that Revelation is not often allegory as we know it—where one thing simply represents another. It is more often a rich, multi-faceted vision with overlaid and overlapping images which convey multiple meanings at the same time. Jesus wants us to engage our imaginations, and not treat these visions like a cypher to be decoded.

• **Why does John react as he does?** So much is lost. He has seen the glory of God in heaven and God holds out his purposes for history, ready to go, as it were. But no-one is able to unfold God's purposes in history. History, it seems, is left to spin out of control. The harmony of creation in chapter 4 is left behind to be replaced by the chaos of history. John sees the mess of the world, and there is no one to sort it out.

7. How do the descriptions of the Lamb in verses 6-8 build to show us who John is talking about? The Lion of Judah and the Root of David are allusions to Genesis 49 v 9-10 and Isaiah 11 v 1-10. This is the promised messianic King, who restores the kingdom of God. He is a Lion, and a slaughtered Lamb. He is a King and a sacrifice. He has seven horns: he is perfectly powerful. He has seven eyes: he sees everything perfectly. The seven spirits (the Holy Spirit) are intimately connected with him.

8. The song in v 9-10 explains how the Lamb became worthy. What did he do and for whom? He died to redeem his people.

• **What makes the Lamb different to the rulers and leaders who might be found in an earthly throne room, presidential palace or a parliament?** Instead of the mighty creatures of imperial power, we have a Lamb. Instead of a victorious general, we have one who has been slain. Instead of the power, glory and wisdom of empire, we have the weakness, shame and folly of the cross (1 Corinthians 1 v 18 – 2 v 5). But it's the folly and weakness of the cross that has conquered. The King reigns from the cross. The Lamb has all strength (seven horns), all knowledge (seven eyes), and is all present (the seven spirits or sevenfold Spirit). We worship the King who was slain and who has conquered through death. Conquering through death is the paradigm of how Christians should respond to empire. The emotional force of chapter 5 is that conquering through death is real victory.

9. What is the overwhelming response in v 11-14 to what the Lamb has done? The Lamb receives the acclamation of heaven. All creation takes up the refrain in verses 13-14. This is not a trick of words. This is reality. The "failure" of the cross has turned out to be the turning point of history and is the focus of heaven's worship. Suffering leads to victory.

10. APPLY: How might you explain the essence of the Christian message to people from just these two chapters of Revelation? Chapters 4 and 5 show us the divine drama from a cosmic perspective. God is our Creator. Christ is worthy to reign because he was slain, and that reign takes place through the mission of the church. Mission is the meaning of the cross.

11. APPLY: What do verses 9-10 tell us about who the gospel is for, and what our mission is as Christians?

• *Christ died for every people group.* Christ died so that there might be people from every people group among his people. Mission to the ends of the earth is the outworking of the cross. Think about the language of "purchase". Christ has purchased specific people from every nation, and so they now belong to him. Our job is to gather them. Our commission is not just to make disciples; it is to make disciples from every nation. If we're content to leave unreached people unreached, then we've missed the point of the atonement.

• *Christ died to make us missionaries.* Christ died to make us "a kingdom and priests" (v 10). It is an allusion to the missional identity of Israel (Exodus 19 v 4-6). Israel was to make God known to the world as a light to the nations. John says Christians are now that priestly kingdom. Christ died to make us a missionary people. So, if we are content to leave people unreached, we've missed the point of the atonement. Reaching the unreached peoples of the world is a task Christ has given to the church. It's not simply a problem for mission agencies. It's a challenge for you. What are you going to do about it?

4 Revelation 6 – 11
THE CHAOS OF HISTORY

THE BIG IDEA
In the here and now there is chaos—warfare, disease, suffering and death. But these are not signs that God is absent, or that he has abandoned his people. They are signs that God is in control, because history is working its way towards fulfilling God's purposes.

SUMMARY
It's best to see this section of Revelation as a whole series of overlapping visions. The seals on the mysterious scroll are opened. But before the final seventh seal is opened, there is a sequence of seven trumpets. The theme is revisited in chapter 16, when seven bowls are poured out. Accompanying each of these is a disaster. One thing to note is that these appear to get worse with each cycle: with the seals a quarter of the earth is affected; with the trumpets, a third of the earth. In 10 v 3-4, seven thunders are announced, but they are not described. Perhaps they would have affected half the earth. The seven bowls of chapters 15-16 affect *everyone*.

Some ways of reading Revelation suggest that we should view these events as consecutive sequences that describe "the end times" leading up to the return of Christ and the last judgment. In this study, we adopt a different view. We need to read Revelation not as a sequential list of events, but as a series of parallel pictures that are designed to stir our imaginations. It's as though John is saying: *It's a bit like this, or a bit like that; or perhaps it will help to think of it in this way.* This is a long section of the book, so encourage your group to dwell not

so much on the detail but on the big picture. And keep taking them back to the central situation that God's people faced, and we face still. Our experience of life is chaotic. A conflict breaks out; a pandemic strikes panic into us all; there are famines and water shortages, droughts and famine; there are political reversals and unexpected outcomes. We are tempted to think that God is not in control, or that history has lost its way. But the key thing to note here is that all the chaos on earth is enacted from heaven. It is the Lamb—Jesus—who breaks the seals. It is the angels—servants of God—who blow the trumpets and pour out the bowls. These things are to be expected because they are part of God's purposes for the world.

In general, the first five elements of each series of seven relate to the realities of history. Number 6 points to what will happen at the end of history. Number 7 portrays what happens beyond. If you keep this pattern in mind, it is easier to see how these sequences fit together.

See *Revelation For You* for a fuller description of the questions surrounding interpretation of Revelation.

In chapters 10 and 11 the pictures change, and focus more on the experience of being part of God's people in the chaos of history. Through the images of a little scroll that John eats (chapter 10);,and the imagery around the two witnesses in chapter 11, we see a picture of what it is like to be a faithful witness to Christ. It is to bear the gospel message to others, even if this means rejection by the world, suffering and death. Mirroring Ezekiel's call to ministry, John must swallow the scroll (v 10), which is both as sweet as honey, but bitter in the stomach. We love the gospel message, but it drives us to action.

OPTIONAL EXTRA

Revelation is about encouraging us to see the chaotic events of world and personal history from heaven's perspective. One old illustration for this is of a tapestry, where we see the back as a chaotic mixture of what look like random threads. It is only when you turn the tapestry over that you see the pattern they are creating. *Either*: Google some pictures of the back and front of a tapestry. Print them out and show them to the group, asking, "What is this a picture of?" *Or*: find a website or photos of close-up pictures, and play a game of guessing what something is from close up.

GUIDANCE FOR QUESTIONS

1. What are the biggest, most shocking events in world news that you have ever experienced? How did you feel as you heard of them, or watched them unfold on the news? For older people in your group it might be the Cuba missile crisis, the moon landing, or the assassination of President Kennedy. For younger people it might be a terror attack like 9/11 or 7/7, an unexpected election outcome, exam results or announcing the winner of *Big Brother* or *America's got Talent*.

2. The first four seals: What do each of these four horsemen do (v 1-6)? How many people are affected? This might seem very distant to those of us living in modern, peaceful democracies. But perhaps we are too optimistic about our ability to propagate such peace throughout the world through aid and military intervention. In many parts of the world still today we see external conquest (v 1-3), internal conflict (v 3-4), famine with rampant inflation (v 5-6), and widespread death (v 7-8).

- **How does the colour of each horse reflect the activity of its rider?** White suggests conquest (in the same way a white flag symbolises surrender), red suggests blood, black suggests death, and the pale horse suggests a sick complexion or a corpse.

3. What repeated phrase (v 2, 4 and 8) makes it clear who is in charge? The Lamb opens the seals: It is Jesus who is in charge of all these things. The way it is expressed here shows that they are the result of what some might call his "permissive will". He opens the seals and gives power to the horsemen to unleash their horrors on a restricted portion of the world's population. Even as these consequences of the fall are permitted to rage throughout the world, their effect is moderated and held back from what it might be. It is the same principle we see outlined in Job chapters 1 and 2.

4. The fifth seal: What is the significance of who we see in verse 9 and where they are? Martyred Christians are seen under an altar in heaven. Heaven was often seen in Jewish thought as the temple of God (e.g. Habakkuk 2 v 20). Indeed, Hebrews 9 says the earthly temple was a copy of the heavenly one. The altar shows that the deaths of the martyrs are seen by God as a sacrifice. They're not simply murders, but offerings to God (2 Timothy 4 v 6). The martyrs are given a white robe, symbolising their vindication and victory. The world made a judgment against them, but God makes a counter-judgment for them.

- **What do they pray for (v 10), and what must they wait for (v 11)?** "How long?" they cry. But the time has not yet come. There are more martyrs to come. It's a reminder that we are still at war. These chapters are Jesus' propaganda poster, powerfully reminding Christians that we need to live on a war footing. The weapons of the martyrs in this war are "the word of God and the testimony they had maintained" (Revelation 6 v 9).

5. What event is portrayed when the sixth seal is opened (v 12-17)? The sixth seal is about the end of the world, the judgment of God on the wicked and the vindication of God's people.

- **What two reactions are there to this event (v 10, implied, and 15-17)?** The faithful long for it. Those who oppose God will flee in terror but find no place to hide.

6. What is the implied answer to the haunting question in verse 17? No one. It is clear that when the sixth seal is opened (= when Christ returns in judgment), all who have rejected and opposed him will fall. Judgment will be so terrible that people wish that they were crushed by a rockfall, rather than face the Living God.

7. APPLY: How was this picture of the world under the four horsemen accurate then, and how has it played out throughout history? What about now? Very accurate. War, death and disease have been variable but constant companions of the human race. As military technology has got more sophisticated, our ability to kill in large numbers has grown. We might be tempted to think that many of the world's problems have been solved. There have not been any major world wars in the last 75 years, and health and life expectancy are

rising. And yet there are still a billion people living in poverty, and there are growing concerns over famine, water shortages and global pandemics. It is rather ironic that the invention of weapons of mass destruction (nerve agents and atomic weapons) have actually had a repressive effect on deaths from conventional warfare. But there remains an uneasy atmosphere in world affairs. The horsemen still ride the earth.

- **What should the implications be for us as we witness war, disaster, famine or unrest at home or in other countries?** We should not be thrown by them. Disasters like this do not suggest that God is not there, or that God is not concerned. They should be signs to believers that history is moving forward to its ultimate goal: the return of the Lord Jesus and the just judgment of all humankind. It is not uncommon to struggle with the idea that God is sovereign over these things. If anyone is grappling with this, suggest they read *How could God let that happen?* by Christopher Ash (TGBC, 2017).

EXPLORE MORE
Read Revelation 7. How do we know that the number of people "sealed" is symbolic (v 4-8, 9)? God is at work gathering his people from the four corners of the earth. The countless multitude (v 9) shows that these numbers are metaphorical, and not, as the Jehovah's Witnesses teach, literal. The point is that God's followers are known and numbered. They will all be gathered and marked or "sealed" by the Holy Spirit so that none will be lost by an administrative error. The number should evoke not fear at being excluded but confidence that, if we belong to Christ, we are utterly safe and will not be forgotten. **What is the significance of their clothes, and how have they got to a place of**

safety? They wear the white robes of the righteousness of Christ, and carry palm branches of victory. Though they have endured suffering, hostility and martyrdom, and remained faithful through it all, they know who gets the praise and glory for everything: "Salvation belongs to our God!" They know that despite the immense effort it took to remain faithful, it is by grace alone that they are saved. Washing something in blood doesn't usually make it white. But that is precisely what the Lamb's blood achieves for those who trust him. The only way to have the "right clothes" for heaven is to ask Jesus to wash our dirt away through his death on the cross. Jesus' story in Matthew 22 v 1-14 makes exactly the same point. Sometimes it feels that being rejected for having the wrong "clothes" is somehow unfair. It is not. Only the pure and holy can enter the eternal presence of the pure and holy God. And we can only be made pure and holy through the gift of God to us of Jesus' perfect righteousness.

What blessings do God's people enjoy, both now and in eternity? Security. Confidence. Forgiveness. Assurance that God will never let us go.

8. Who do you think the two witnesses represent (also referred to as olive trees and lampstands, v 4)? The two witnesses of verse 3 are God's people: his royal priesthood. Mission is both a priestly activity (representing God to the world) and a royal activity (extending Christ's reign by calling on people to submit to his authority). And through our words we bring the fire of divine judgment on those who reject our message (see 2 Corinthians 2 v 15-16).

• **What power has God given to them? What does this remind you of from the Old Testament?** To our priestly and kingly roles, we can add a prophetic role since the two witnesses are also an allusion to two of the greatest figures of the Old Testament: Moses (who turned water to blood) and Elijah (who prayed and stopped the rain). Today, we are engaged in powerful word-ministry. For we bring either eternal life or eternal death as we proclaim the gospel. But we should not expect people to like us for it!

9. What happens to them, and how do the people react (v 9-10)? They are killed by the beast from the Abyss—a reference to Satan, perhaps through his influence and control of the persecuting state. The people around treat these murders like Christmas—they throw a party and exchange presents over the dead bodies.

10. What happens next, and how do the people react (v 11-12)? The resurrection of the witnesses in verses 11-12 should not be understood as literal. It presents the truth of history as a whole: the church is persecuted, Christians are martyred, and at times the cause of Christ seems defeated. But the church survives and comes back with renewed strength, and the cause of Christ continues. What is God's "secret weapon" in the face of the hostile powers of this world? It is the faithful people of God, sustained by the powerful Spirit of God. Again and again throughout history regimes have arisen and it's looked as if they would wipe out the church. But those regimes have gone, and the church has come through persecution stronger. It has been victorious through suffering. Life has come through death.

• **Where do the witnesses end up?** Ultimately, faithful Christians end up alive in heaven; those who oppose them remain in the earthly city, which is still under God's judgment, as indicated by the earthquake.

11. What happens in response to the miracle of the raising of the witnesses? What is the significance of that?

The calamities of the seven seals and seven trumpets do not bring repentance (Revelation 9 v 20-21). Instead, the nations fear God and give him glory in response to the faithful witness of God's people—especially their faithful witness "even to the point of death" (2 v 10). Or perhaps sometimes it's the suffering witness of God's people combined with the calamities of history that brings people to repentance. The turmoil of history on its own, represented by the seven seals and trumpets, leads only to judgment. But the turmoil of history combined with Christian witness leads some to repentance.

12. APPLY: Who are you fearful of sharing the gospel with? What makes you hesitant? Sharing Jesus can lead us into conflict or provoke the hatred or dismissal of others. We prefer comfortable lives, or the approval of others, rather than the approval of God and the deferred pleasures of eternity with Christ.

- **What encouragement to persevere with gospel proclamation have you seen in this section of Revelation?** We must remember what is at stake: heaven and hell. We must remember what we owe: everything to Jesus who died to bring us forgiveness. We must remember that the route to glory is through suffering. We must remember that we must expect opposition. Above all, we must remember that God alone is worthy of praise and honour.

5 Revelation 12 – 16
WHO DO YOU WORSHIP?

THE BIG IDEA

Christians live in cultures that demands obedience, using a mix of threats and seduction to draw us away from Christ. Satanic influence is behind this.

SUMMARY

In the first 11 chapters of Revelation the key question is: "What do you see?" In chapters 12 – 14, the question changes to "Who do you worship?" As with the rest of Revelation, help the group to see that what John presents us with are overlapping visions of the same thing, seen from different perspectives. The gospel story is told in different ways that might seem unfamiliar to us. This study focuses on chapters 12 and 13—which present our current and future situation using two images. In the first, a woman who is God's servant, gives birth to the Saviour and then gives birth to numerous other offspring—the church. The dragon (Satan) seeks to destroy the woman and the child (Jesus), but they are protected. Frustrated and enraged, he stalks the earth seeking to destroy the church. But the woman and her offspring are protected and kept safe by God.

Following these visions, there are others. Chapter 14 has fresh visions of the Lamb, the 144,000, messages from three angels about God's judgment and Christ's care for his beleaguered people, and a call to remain faithful. Chapters 15 – 16 is another cycle of seven plagues poured into and then out of bowls onto the earth.

Throughout each of these sections, there is a constant comparison between those who worship the beast and those who worship the Lamb. We are told again and again that the beast and all those who worship it will end in ruin. And we are told that the lived reality of those who worship the Lamb will be one of struggle and suffering, as the devil and the agents of his work, the beast and the false prophet—and other symbolic representations of a human culture hostile to God and the gospel—work to compromise or destroy believers. But ultimately their destiny is glory. And the route to glory, like that of their Saviour, is through suffering. There is also a constant reiteration of the themes of Revelation: the Lamb is control; the devil is defeated; judgment is certain; the chaos of history is within God's control. And the call is repeated again and again: remain faithful, bear your testimony, do not be convinced by the lies of the beast, and preach the gospel whatever happens.

OPTIONAL EXTRA

Play a board or card game that involves threat and reward. It could be something as simple as *Jenga*, or *Operation*, with a prize for winning, and a "punishment" for losing. This introduces the general theme of the study.

GUIDANCE FOR QUESTIONS

1. Do you know anyone who has given up being a Christian? What happened, and what do you think lay behind that decision? People fall away for all kinds of reasons, but most often it is because they have found something that they love enough to compromise over—their career or work, a spouse or children, a hobby or pursuit. It is rare that people walk away from faith because of intellectual objections, although that may be used as an excuse. When people face hostility or challenge, that is the moment that these fault lines in their faith tend to appear.

• **When have you have been most tempted to give up? What happened, and how did you hang on?** Allow people to share honestly about the things they have struggled with. This is not the moment to speak to any faith struggles people may have had, or have now. The study will do that. But do note down anything that you think requires follow up in the future—perhaps one to one.

2. Who do the characters in the story represent, and what is their motivation? (Hint: There may be more than one answer for the woman.) The woman *could* be Mary since she gives birth to Jesus. But she's more likely to be the people of God as a whole. Isaiah portrays Israel as a woman in childbirth, waiting to bring forth the Messiah and the woman in Revelation spans the whole history of redemption. Revelation 12 v 17 refers to Christians as "the rest of her offspring"—the product of the mission of the church. The child is Jesus. Verse 5 quotes Psalm 2 v 9, where God's Messiah receives an iron sceptre to rule the nations. The dragon is Satan (v 9), and is portrayed as terrifyingly dangerous: strong, clever, murderous and with enormous power. But his vindictive power is chanelled through the mechanisms of state. It is dramatic, but correct to describe regimes as satanic when they attempt to suppress the word of God, the gospel, and to persecute God's people.

3. What does the dragon try to do to the child and the woman's other offspring, and how is he thwarted? He attempts to murder the child, and so thwart God's plan of redemption. When this fails, he does his level best to threaten and destroy the "other children", the church. But God protects them, and the scene ends with the dragon standing on the seashore breathing threats and fire, but, ultimately, unable to do anything.

• **What incidents in the life of Christ and the church does this remind you of?** Verses 1-5 refer to the first coming of Jesus seen as a single event, encompassing his birth, the cross (Satan's attempt to devour the child) and his resurrection and ascension (the child being snatched up to heaven). Throughout history Satan has opposed God's people, and sought to destroy them.

4. When does the angelic war in verses 7-9 take place? What do you think it refers to? Job 1 suggests that before the coming of Jesus, Satan had access to heaven, and what he did in heaven was accuse God's people. But he and his angels have now "lost their place in heaven"—that is, Satan can no longer accuse us because God's people are now righteous through the death and resurrection of Jesus. We shouldn't focus on Satan's location, for the spatial imagery of being in heaven is used in Revelation 12 metaphorically to describe Satan's power to accuse. The thing to focus on is that the coming of Jesus, and in particular his death and resurrection, has changed the nature of the heavens and the earth for ever.

• **What can Satan no longer do, according to verse 10? Why?** Satan can no longer accuse because God's

people are now righteous through the death and resurrection of Jesus. Satan is defeated through the cross. The verdict has been given in the court of heaven. The prosecution case is rejected and the prosecution counsel is silenced. Only the defence counsel remains—Jesus our advocate (Romans 8 v 34). The defendant is declared not guilty. There is no condemnation (Romans 8 v 1). The archangel Michael is simply the bailiff carrying out the eviction order that was secured at the cross. If Satan had been victorious, then the saints would have been cast out of heaven, because his accusations against us would have been vindicated. But Christ is victorious, so it's Satan who is cast out and we who are vindicated in Christ. Satan loses his "place" (Revelation 12 v 8) because we have gained a place.

5. What is Satan doing now according to verses 13-17? Verses 12-13 tell us that Satan has been thrown down to earth in a great rage. He is doomed but still dangerous, like a defeated army that is in full retreat and yet doing its best to inflict whatever damage it can on the victors. And the focus is on "the word of ... testimony" that is given by God's people. It is the testimony—the gospel—that draws others into Christ's forgiveness. And it is the faithful bearing of that testimony through persecution and suffering that brings the saints, like their saviour, to heaven at last.

6. APPLY: How should Christians therefore think about Satan, the church, and our own discipleship? We should not underestimate his power and intent. He is an enraged, dangerous, mortally damaged dragon that would love to destroy and devour anyone he can (see 1 Peter 5 v 8).

But nor should we overestimate him. His claws have been drawn. His chief weapons are lies and fear. But he cannot harm us if we remain faithful to Jesus. Revelation 12 reminds us that Satan is both a real and a defeated foe. Both truths should motivate us. The one command in the chapter is in verse 12: "Rejoice!" There is no place for apathy and there is no need for despair.

EXPLORE MORE

Read 1 Kings 19 v 1-8. How does Revelation 12 allude to this story, and to Israel's 40 years in the wilderness? What does it show us about God's care for us? The narrative in verses 13-17 picks up on images from the exodus, and the story of Elijah, who fled from Jezebel. God keeps his people for a symbolic 42 months before they inherit the promised new creation (v 14). God's people are a wilderness people, not at home in a hostile world. But in the "wilderness" we are nourished and kept by God, just as Israel was nourished by manna and protected by the pillars of cloud and fire. God lovingly cares for and protects his people.

7. What do you think the two beasts represent, from their description? The beasts together represent the political and military power of empire. In John's case, this was seen in the arrival of Roman armies from across the Mediterranean to conquer Asia Minor. The ten horns, seven heads and ten crowns are a reworking of the images in Daniel 7, in which Daniel saw successive empires. Here is the latest expression of imperial power. It looks like various fierce carnivores—animals used by Rome to signify its power. Although the image of the beasts portrays the Roman Empire then, it could be applied to any empire throughout history.

• **What does the first beast do, and how does the world respond to it?** Not all power is bad and not all empires are evil. But this empire utters "blasphemies" (v 5-6). It takes the place of God, redefines morality and demands ultimate allegiance (v 8).

8. What is confusing about the description of the second beast in verse 11? The second beast looks like a lamb—innocent and harmless, in a twisted parody of Jesus. But it speaks the words of the dragon, Satan.

• **How does it secure its following?** The second beast is the propagandist. It is not providing a reasoned case for empire, or wielding a stick to threaten. It produces signs and images to seduce, threaten, impress and overwhelm the peoples of the earth (v 13-15). The Roman Empire exercised control not only through military power but through access to its prosperity. "Soft power", we would call it today, or "winning hearts and minds".

9. How do the two beasts combine to oppress people—and God's people in particular? Because the beasts demand allegiance, this inevitably brings them into conflict with God's people, for we have a competing allegiance. So they wage war against the church (v 7). The results are inevitable: Christians will be imprisoned and martyred (v 9-10). The two beasts show two sides of how dominating cultures shape their citizens, using both carrot and stick: acquiesce, and you can share in the bounty; resist, and you're excluded. John's vision invites us to question the propaganda of the second beast and see through its images. All its wonders are a parody of God's. It makes fire come down from heaven (v 13). like Elijah (1 Kings 18). It performs signs and wonders (Revelation 13 v 14).

just as Jesus and the apostles did. It exalts the beast who was wounded and yet lives just as Christians exalt the Lamb who was slain but rose again. The triumvirate of the dragon and the two beasts form a parody of the Trinity. Through a thousand adverts and glossy magazines the beast says, *All this could be yours if you bow before me.* John wants us to see the work of the second beast for what it is. He wants us to reject its seductions and worship Christ instead.

10. What do you think the significance is of the marking on the forehead or hand (v 16)? A mark is a sign of ownership—just as Jesus marks or "seals" his people with his Holy Spirit to show's his mark of ownership (Revelation 7 v 4; 14 v 1; Ephesians 1 v 13-14; 2 Corinthians 1: 21-22). The point is not to look for literal marks today (like bar codes, or embedded chips). The point is that the beast demands our allegiance, and wants to "own" us.

• **What, do you think, is the significance of the number 666 (v 18)?** There are many theories. One is that 666 is the sum of Nero's name in a Hebrew system in which letters were assigned numeric values. If so, John is saying the wise person realises Nero and his successors are the latest manifestation of satanic power. Alternatively, it may represent one less than the perfection represented by 777. If so, John is saying that the wise person recognises imperial power is not good nor the final word in history. It portrays itself as perfection, but constantly falls short.

EXPLORE MORE
Read Ephesians 1 v 13-14; 4 v 30. How does God mark or "seal" those who belong to him? How do we know we are sealed? The mark of the Spirit in someone's life is a new desire to love others,

to call God Father to want to grow more like Christ. In Revelation's terms, it will involve the instinct to be faithful to God under pressure, and to bear the testimony of Jesus.

11. APPLY: Where do you see the beasts at work in the world today? It's easy to see the first beast: in North Korea, Pakistan, Iran and many other parts of the world where being "out" as a Christian puts you in the firing line. But the second beast is much more subtle. His influence is everywhere in our culture—urging people just to "fit in" and belong. Our cultures excite people about the value of belonging, and astonish people with technological wonders, or attractively made films.

12. APPLY: In what practical ways can we help each other to resist the hostility and seduction of our world? The answer must include reminding ourselves and each other about: the glory and greatness of Jesus; the reality of the coming judgment and our vindication by God; and the wonder of the new creation in which God will "wipe away every tear". In practical terms this will involve: keeping ourselves close to God and to each other; reading his word; putting ourselves under regular teaching and preaching; and engaging perceptively with the world, politics and culture through the lens of Scripture. The most obvious places where we feel this pressure are at work and in education.

6
Revelation 17 – 20
THE JUSTICE OF THE LAMB

THE BIG IDEA

The glittering, powerful, immensely wealthy culture of Rome is revealed for what it truly is: evil; opposed to God and his people; motivated by Satan. But God's judgment is coming and will be terrible, final, complete and utterly fair.

SUMMARY

John's overlapping visions continue. The first is of a woman who rides on the back of a great beast (a different image to the beasts of chapter 13). She is the great prostitute—Babylon, the great mother of prostitutes (17 v 5-6). Enormously wealthy, completely immoral and hideously bloodthirsty, she devours nations and people, and, in particular, destroys Christians. But the whole point of chapter 17 is to reveal that her days are numbered. The description is a thinly-veiled reference to Rome. The beast she rides on and the waters that surround her are clear references to the geography and history of Rome. It is no wonder John has been exiled to Patmos! He predicts that the Lamb will destroy both beast and prostitute (v 14). In a change of focus, he also predicts that Rome will be destroyed by the nations that it once subjugated (v 15-18).

Chapter 18 describes both the joy and the lamenting of those who watch as Babylon (= Rome = any culture that is hostile to God) burns under God's judgment. Judgment will divide the world into two and reveal where our true attachments are. Those who love the world will weep at its passing. Those whose hope is in the world to come will rejoice.

Chapter 19 picks up the imagery of chapter 13 and describes the end of the beast and the false prophet (the second beast). They are thrown into the lake of fire (v 20), an image of judgment and hell, by a rider on a white horse, whose description makes clear that this is Jesus.

Chapter 20 may be controversial for your group, because it describes "the millennium"—the thousand years during which Christ reigns on earth. Christians have understood this image in different ways, some thinking it refers to a literal reign for a literal thousand years, others thinking it is metaphorical of the age when Jesus rules through his people (the church), i.e. now. These notes have assumed the latter, but you will want to be sensitive to those in the group who may have other views. The passage finishes with a vivid description of the judgment—everyone is raised to life again; everyone has one of two destinies. The key issue is whether our names are written in the Lamb's book of life.

OPTIONAL EXTRA

Play a game that involves waiting and tension, like Pass the Bomb. Or search online for "The Marshmallow Test" and show a video of children having to choose whether to wait to eat a marshmallow with the promise of a greater future reward.

GUIDANCE FOR QUESTIONS

1. Have you ever had to wait a long time for something? How did you feel during that time? It could be waiting for Christmas as a child, for exam results, for someone to die, or until your wedding day. There are many emotions: anxiety, excitement, fear, frustration, and nervous dread that it will not happen or the result will be worse than you hope or expect. No need to comment here; just set the scene for what it is like to wait, and the understandable emotions involved.

2. What clues are there in this hideous description as to what the figures of the beast and the woman represent?
The world of Revelation was a world of cities, as it is for us. And cities were often personified as women. Rome was personified as the goddess Roma and this is how she was worshipped in Asia Minor, where John's readers lived. But in Revelation she appears not as a goddess but as a prostitute (v 1) who seduces the world, drawing people into her idolatry (v 2). The fact that John is introduced to her by one of the angels who had one of the bowls suggests we are about to see the reason for God's wrath. Babylon persecutes God's people (v 6). She is the manifestation of the power of the dragon, the beast and the false prophet (v 3). A name or mark on the forehead in Revelation indicates a person's true character and hers is clear. She is the "mother of prostitutes" because her children (her inhabitants) share her spiritual adultery.

3. What is John's reaction to this vision, and what's the reaction of those who are not saved (v 6, 8)? John, it seems, is astonished by this vision, probably in dread, though possibly with attraction—we have already noted the dissonance in this image: a beautiful, bejewelled, beguiling woman with ruthless, bloody intent. But John's angelic guide will expose her false glory. The unsaved are astonished too—but perhaps with adoration at the strength and power of the beast and the woman.

• **What is your reaction?** Think of John's description of Babylon the Prostitute in terms of a political cartoonist presenting an exaggerated personification of the city to satirise her pompous claims. Think of a bloated Britannia or Uncle Sam squashing the British lion or American eagle on which they sit. This is the kind of imagery that is evoked in this powerful word picture.

4. What is meant by the repeated phrase "once was, now is not, and yet will come..." (v 7, 8)? Twice in Revelation 17 v 7-8 we're told the beast "once was, now is not, and yet will come." In other words, the beast manifests itself in one form. This then passes away and "is not". Throughout history the beast returns in other guises. Kingdoms come and seem utterly solid for a time, and yet they decline and fall. This phrase is another parody of the living God "who is and who was and who is to come" (1 v 8; 4 v 8; 11 v 16; 16 v 5). The Roman Empire was one of a long line of many others. But it fell, and new empires arose, including ours. But God always is.

5. What becomes of the beast and the woman in the end (v 10-12, 16)? They are destroyed by a toxic mixture of internal strife and external rebellion. In 17:10-12 the angel speaks of coming kings and transfers of power. The details may be confusing to us, but if we step back, the bigger picture is clear. In Daniel 7 the same language is used to describe successive empires. So the symbolic numbers seven and ten in Revelation 17 v 3 and 10-12 probably don't refer to specific kings. Instead John is highlighting the way the beast manifests its power in recurring political empires and systems throughout history. For example, Domitian (probably the Emperor when John was writing) was regarded as a second Nero.

So these chapters speak simultaneously to the specific situation of first-century Rome and to every age. Though the woman "rides" on the beast and "rules" over kings (v 7, 18), in verse 16 they turn on her and destroy her. The city of Rome will be destroyed by the very empire it built in fulfilment of God's word of judgment (v 17). The allegiance of Rome's client rulers is an act of self-interest and, when the political climate shifts, they will be quick to switch that allegiance. This is precisely what happened in AD 410 when Rome was sacked by people it had once ruled.

6. APPLY: What do you find most attractive and enjoyable about the modern world we live in? Our world is truly astonishing. Its achievements are immense, its technology miraculous; its abilities seemingly endless, its wealth staggering. No wonder we are beguiled by the bright lights and enjoyments it offers.

7. APPLY: How can you enjoy these blessings without being consumed by them?
Understanding this vision will make a crucial difference between the astonishment of the faithful saints, and the astonishment of those who have not had their names written in the book of life from before the creation of the world. We recognise that the world is, at the end of the day, a prostitute whose calls we must resist. There is only one destiny for those who follow her. We fix our eyes on a different prize.

EXPLORE MORE
Read Revelation 18. What is the verdict of heaven (v 4-8)? We discover the fall of Rome will be an act of divine judgment on her economic injustice and exploitation. Her judgment is just. The word "double" in

verse 6 is better translated "duplicate". Her judgment duplicates her crimes (v 6-7).
18 v 4 commands Christians to "come out of her". What do you think this might mean in practice? The command is not talking about a geographical movement. There's no suggestion they go into exile or create a ghetto in the hills. Elsewhere they are called to a suffering witness in the midst of Rome. No, instead he's calling for an ideological movement. Jesus wants us to adopt a different set of values, a different set of priorities, a different allegiance, a different object of worship. God is not against trade and commerce in themselves. But he does calls us to be separate from injustice. If there is a geographic movement, it's one that takes place within the imagination: we move from citizenship on earth to citizenship in heaven. We pack our bags, leave our home in Babylon the Prostitute and set out for a new home in Jerusalem the Bride.

8. What invitation are we given in v 5?
We are called to sing praise to God (v 5) for his acts of judgment and salvation. Every act in the drama of the book of Revelation is accompanied by worship in heaven, and 17 v 1 – 19 v 10 is no different. Its focus has been on earth, but its climax is in heaven. In 19 v 5 we're invited to join this song of praise. Whether we choose to mourn or sing reveals our ultimate allegiance.

9. How should Christians respond to seeing both salvation and judgment?
By rejoicing. This may feel odd to us, but it is a theme throughout Scripture that judgment, even though it is described in horrific terms, is not something that the people of God will find abhorrent, but will rejoice in. The right thing will have been done by a righteous God.

10. What invitation are we given in verse 9? What does this mean? The song of heaven turns into the second invitation—an invitation to the marriage feast of the Lamb. Instead of receiving an invitation from a prostitute, we're invited to be the bride of God's Son. Instead of a woman clothed in the purple of empire (17 v 4), we see a bride clothed in the fine linen of righteous deeds (19 v 8). Instead of an invitation to immorality (17 v 2), we're invited to a marriage (19 v 7).

In 19 v 9 the angel says to John, "Write this". John presumably has been feverishly scribbling down everything he's seen and heard. But this part of the vision must not be missed: "Blessed are those who are invited to the wedding supper of the Lamb!" So great and gracious is this message that the angel feels compelled to add, '"These are the true words of God". In other words, *I'm not making this up!*

11. How does verse 10 underline the response we are called to make? John is overwhelmed by what he has seen, and the greatness and graciousness of the invitation he has received. His understandable response is to fall before the angel who delivers the message. But he is sharply rebuked. Only God is to be worshipped!

12. APPLY: What are the signs that someone has accepted the invitation to the marriage feast of the Lamb? Praise and glory given to God and performing righteous deeds (v 8).

EXPLORE MORE
Read Revelation 20 v 1-6. What explanations have you heard about the meaning of the millennium pictured in these verses? These verses not only describe a battle but have been a battlefield

of debate between Christians over the years. There are different ways of reading these chapters of Revelation, depending on whether you take them to be describing a sequential series of events that take place in the future, or symbolic of something that is happening throughout history. There are three main views (with many variations):

Premillennialism: Premillennialists believe that Christ will return pre- (before) the millennium. He will then reign on earth for a literal thousand-year period. When Christ returns, deceased Christians will be raised, and those believers who haven't died will be given resurrection bodies. Christ will be physically present on earth and reign as its King, bringing peace and prosperity, with believers reigning alongside him. Unbelievers will continue to live on earth and many, though not all, will turn to Christ. The thousand-year reign of Christ will end with the great battle of Armageddon, after which the final judgment will take place. Premillennialists tend to interpret Old Testament promises of the restoration of the land of Israel as pointing to the millennial reign of Christ on earth.

Postmillennialism: Postmillennialists believe that Christ returns post- (after) the millennium. They believe the millennium is a future golden age of gospel advance in which the church grows and exercises a positive influence in society. After this golden age, Christ will return and the final judgment will take place. Postmillennialists generally have a positive view of history. History is improving as the gospel advances.

Amillennialism: The prefix "a-" is somewhat misleading as it could imply a belief that there is no millennium. But amillennialists do believe there is a millennium. But it's not in the future. Instead they see the millennium as describing the present age of the church. The millennium is therefore the period between the first and second comings of Christ. Amillennialists interpret Revelation 20 in the light of the broader picture presented in the Scriptures.

What response do you think we should make as we read these words? Surely John would not want our response to be arguing about the detail! The big-picture teaching and responses are:

• *Confidence:* God is more powerful than Satan. At every moment in this narrative, God is in control.

• *Privilege:* Those who belong to Christ reign with Christ. We are encouraged to remain faithful and to resist worshipping the beast because of our status.

• *Perseverance:* Even those who have been beheaded for remaining faithful to Christ will reign with him (v 4). We are encouraged to bear the testimony of Jesus and the word of God.

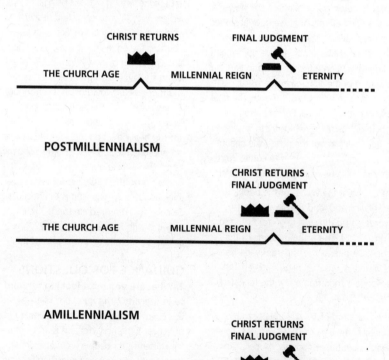

PREMILLENNIALISM

CHRIST RETURNS   FINAL JUDGMENT

THE CHURCH AGE   MILLENNIAL REIGN   ETERNITY

POSTMILLENNIALISM

CHRIST RETURNS
FINAL JUDGMENT

THE CHURCH AGE   MILLENNIAL REIGN   ETERNITY

AMILLENNIALISM

CHRIST RETURNS
FINAL JUDGMENT

THE CHURCH AGE = MILLENNIAL REIGN   ETERNITY

7 Revelation 21 – 22
THE REIGN OF THE LAMB

THE BIG IDEA

We will not go to heaven. Heaven will come to us. God will establish his perfect kingdom; the old world will be judged, but those who have been faithful to Christ will enjoy reigning with him for ever.

SUMMARY

John reaches the climax of his book. And what a climax! There are many surprises in these chapters that explode many views of heaven and eternity that we have absorbed from the culture. We will not be ethereal spirits; we will have bodies. We do not go up to heaven; heaven comes down to earth in a uniting of the spiritual and physical realms. We will reign with Christ for ever. The final two chapters of Revelation are also heavily laden with symbols, which try to inspire our imaginations about the riches, the beauty and the glory of the world to come. But they are symbols; the reality will be far greater.

At this point the visions of the book of Revelation end, and they end with these words: "And they will reign for ever and ever" (22:5). This is the message of the book. Despite all the apparent vagaries of history, Christ will reign for ever. The epilogue is then framed by the repeated phrase, "Look, I am coming soon!" (v 7, 12)

The final word of Jesus in the book (and indeed in the Bible) is this: "Yes, I am coming soon". And the response is, "Amen, Come, Lord Jesus" (v 20-21; 1 Corinthians 16:22). Perhaps we can think of this as the final "test" offered by the book of Revelation. Jesus says, "I am coming soon". Do we respond with an enthusiastic "Amen"? Do

we pray this prayer? Do we long for Christ's return? Or are our longings elsewhere? Would we prefer his return to be postponed? If so, then this may be a sign that we need to "come out" of Babylon (Revelation 18:4).

OPTIONAL EXTRA

Try to describe somewhere amazing you have been to without giving people the precise location or any giveaway clues. Try to describe what it was like using all of your senses, not just your eyes. And describe what it made you feel like. For example, "I stood on the edge and was overwhelmed and astonished by how enormous it was; I was scared and excited at the same time, and frightened I would fall in, even though I knew I was safe. The range of colours was remarkable, and changed all the time. The hot sun beat down on me, and the air was hot and dry; the sound of crickets filled my ears." Can people guess where it was (The Grand Canyon)? Guide the discussion to think about how difficult it is to adequately describe something so amazing. This is how it is with Revelation 21 and 22. It is describing something that is indescribable.

GUIDANCE FOR QUESTIONS

1. What are you most looking forward to in eternity? This question will help you check what people's understanding of heaven / the new creation is. It may be very different for people with different life experiences. Some may be looking forward to being reunited with lost loved ones. Some may be hungry to see God's justice on others or vindication for themselves, or an end to the struggle with sin or pain or illness. But all should be longing to see God face to face.

2. What is new, and what has passed away (v 1-4)? Everything is new, including heaven, earth and Jerusalem. The first heaven and the first earth, crying, pain, death and illness have all gone. In the new creation there will be no need for handkerchiefs, hospitals or hearses.

3. What will be at the heart of our experience of eternity (v 5-9)? Our relationship with Jesus. We will be honoured, celebrated and cared for like a bride. We shall each be comforted and showered with grace (v 6). Allow the group to talk about what that will mean to each of them.

• **What is the significance of each element of the description of the new Jerusalem?** The numbers are staggering. The city is 1,400 miles (2250km) square and 1400 miles tall! Everest is 6 miles (9.7km) high. This cube echoes the Most Holy Place in Solomon's temple (1 Kings 6 v 20). The walls are 144 cubits (12 x 12) = 65m. The point is clear: once-persecuted Christians will be eternally secure within these walls. This security is reinforced by the presence of angelic watchmen on every gate (v 12). The jewels reflect the jewels in the breastpiece (ephod) of the high priest (Exodus 28 v 17-20). Each element speaks of immense wealth (the gold floor, the pearl gates) that far exceeds the wealth and value of the trinkets offered by this world.

4. What is not present in the new Jerusalem (v 22-27), and what is the significance of each thing mentioned that will be absent?
1. There is no temple. No need for separation or sacrifice. Everyone has access to the Father and the Son. In fact, the new Jerusalem is described almost like a gigantic Most Holy Place—the place where God dwells. *2. No sun or moon.* We have no need of their light because God is present to light our path. *3. No night / the gates are always open.* In a human city closed gates were necessary to prevent intruders and the dark deeds that were done at night. No need for that, because evil of all kinds has been dealt with. *4. Nothing impure.* Nothing will enter that can spoil it. Although this does speak to judgment, it primarily means that eternity can never be a re-run of the first Eden, which was ruined through the presence of the snake. We can be confident that eternity will be unspoiled for ever.

• **What is the significance of verse 26?** There is no room for sin (v 27) but the glory and wealth of the nations will somehow be brought in and incorporated into the new creation. This means that there is some kind of continuity between old and new creations; and there are redeemable value in aspects of our human art and culture.

5. What is the conclusion to the vision in verse 6? What do you think that will be like? We will reign for ever and ever with Christ. It is hard to know what this will be like, but it will involve engagement and work. Presumably, we will return to the original Genesis mandate to subdue the world (and the universe) and fill it to the praise of God's glory.

6. APPLY: What part of John's vision captures your imagination or speaks to your current challenges? Allow the group to dream big. This passage is meant to arouse our hopes and imagination. Encourage them to speak of how they will find eternity a relief, recompense or joy compared with their current lives.

- **How does this vision of eternity help us persevere when things are hard for us?** When difficulties come—illness, persecution, struggling with sin, old age or just tiredness of the bitterness and pettiness of the world—this is an uplifting vision showing that everything our heart yearns for will be fulfilled in the new creation. All our struggles are worth it.

7. APPLY: How do people come to be in the new creation (v 27), and what does that encourage us to keep doing? Only those whose names are in the Lamb's book of life will be there: those who have received forgiveness through the death of Jesus. It encourages us to:
1. *Keep praying for others.* They will only get to be in the new Jerusalem through God's grace, not their own efforts.
2. *Keep sharing the gospel with everyone.* The repeated theme of Revelation is to bear the testimony of Jesus—not just to hold on to your own belief and trust in Christ, but also to proclaim the good news of God's salvation to others.

EXPLORE MORE
Read Romans 8 v 18-23 and 2 Peter 3 v 10-13. Will creation be renewed or replaced? *Romans 8:* Creation will be liberated from its bondage to decay;its beauty will be restored and its ugliness removed. *2 Peter 3:* This passage seems to suggests the destruction of creation. But then the language of destruction was used of Noah's flood (v 6), when the planet itself was not destroyed. So 2 Peter 3 may describe a processing of purging.' The precise extent and relationship of renewal and/or replacement remains a mystery. In resurrection there is both continuity and

discontinuity; the same will be true for creation in general.

8. What phrase is repeated in verses 7 and 12? How could this have been true when John wrote Revelation 2,000 years ago? Jesus is coming "soon". But he has not yet come—after 2,000 years. Christians are meant to live knowing and thinking that Christ will return any moment, and at just the right time. Every day he delays is another day of mercy and gospel opportunity. Every day he delays, more people are being brought into his kingdom. We are called to be patient, and to remember that with the Lord a thousand years are as a day (2 Peter 3 v 8).

9. What are we to think about the teaching in Revelation, and what are we to do with it (v 6-16)?
1. *These words are true (v 6).* John's angelic guide says, "These words are trustworthy and true" because they have come from God. John refers to himself by name (v 9): he heard and saw the visions in this book for himself. This is a first-hand, apostolic report.
2. *These words are to be kept (v 7-9).* Then Jesus himself speaks and calls on us as readers to "[keep] the words". What does this involve? In one sense, all that has been said. But the next incident perhaps highlights the key message. The command is, "Worship God" (v 9). This goes to the core of Revelation. We're to worship God in the face of both the seductions and threat of idolatrous power.
3. *The words are to be read (v 10-11).* Daniel was told to seal up his prophecy for it describes a future time (Daniel 12 v 4, 9). In contrast John is told not to seal the scroll for "the time is near". In other words, this is not a message for some far-off future. This was for John's generation—and therefore is also

for our generation.

4. Continue doing right (v 11). Let wrongdoers continue for their end is coming. Meanwhile, let us continue to do what's right.

10. What final appeal does John want to impress on us (v 17)? *These words are the gospel (v 12-17).* Jesus will reward everyone "according to what they have done" (v 12). So what hope is there for guilty sinners? Our hope is not in our own righteousness. Our hope is in Christ. By faith, we wash our guilty stains in his blood and cloth ourselves with his righteousness. So through Christ the invitation comes to us from the Spirit speaking through the church ("the bride"): he bids us "Come" (v 17).

11. APPLY: Are you more at home in Babylon the Prostitute or Jerusalem the Bride? What are the signs that would show you which is true for you? It can be helpful to talk about dreams and nightmares. If all we are dreaming for is a nice house, nice holidays, nice friends and nice belongings, it tells us something. If our worst nightmare is that our children fail their exams, or our income drops, or our friends reject us for some reason, it tells us something. On the other hand, if we dream of our church growing, our children or grandchildren becoming Christians and gospel workers, our lives honouring Christ and our neighbours hearing the good news, it tells us something different. And if our worst nightmare is that our children reject Christ, or that our church fails and closes, it tells us that our identity and hopes are bound up with Jerusalem the Bride.

12. APPLY: How has God spoken to you through the words of Revelation? What specific steps are you going to take in response? Allow the group time to look back through the studies, and encourage them to come up with one thing that has impressed them most.

Dig deeper with *Revelation For You*

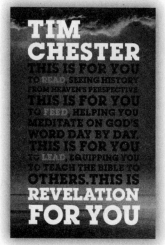

Tim Chester brings his trademark insight and real-world application to the book of Revelation. Written for Christians of every age and stage, whether new believers or pastors and teachers, each title in the series takes a detailed look at a book of the Bible in a readable, relevant way.

Revelation For You is for you:

- **to read**, mapping out the themes, promises and challenges of this book.
- **to feed**, using it as a daily devotional, complete with helpful reflection questions.
- **to lead**, equipping small-group leaders and Bible teachers and preachers to explain, illustrate and apply this wonderful book of the Bible.

Find out more at:
www.thegoodbook.com/for-you

Good Book Guides
The full range

2 Corinthians:
7 Studies
Gary Millar
ISBN: 9781784983895

Galatians: 7 Studies
Timothy Keller
ISBN: 9781908762566

Ephesians: 10 Studies
Thabiti Anyabwile
ISBN: 9781907377099

Ephesians: 8 Studies
Richard Coekin
ISBN: 9781910307694

Philippians: 7 Studies
Steven J. Lawson
ISBN: 9781784981181

Colossians: 6 Studies
Mark Meynell
ISBN: 9781906334246

1 Thessalonians:
7 Studies
Mark Wallace
ISBN: 9781904889533

1&2 Timothy: 7 Studies
Phillip Jensen
ISBN: 9781784980191

Titus: 5 Studies
Tim Chester
ISBN: 9781909919631

Hebrews: 8 Studies
Justin Buzzard
ISBN: 9781906334420

Hebrews: 8 Studies
Michael J. Kruger
ISBN: 9781784986049

James: 6 Studies
Sam Allberry
ISBN: 9781910307816

1 Peter: 6 Studies
Juan R. Sanchez
ISBN: 9781784980177

1 John: 7 Studies
Nathan Buttery
ISBN: 9781904889953

Revelation: 7 Studies
Tim Chester
ISBN: 9781910307021

TOPICAL

Man of God: 10 Studies
Anthony Bewes & Sam Allberry
ISBN: 9781904889977

Biblical Womanhood:
10 Studies
Sarah Collins
ISBN: 9781907377532

The Apostles' Creed:
10 Studies
Tim Chester
ISBN: 9781905564415

Promises Kept: Bible Overview: 9 Studies
Carl Laferton
ISBN: 9781908317933

The Reformation Solas
6 Studies
Jason Helopoulos
ISBN: 9781784981501

Contentment: 6 Studies
Anne Woodcock
ISBN: 9781905564668

Women of Faith:
8 Studies
Mary Davis
ISBN: 9781904889526

Meeting Jesus: 8 Studies
Jenna Kavonic
ISBN: 9781905564460

Heaven: 6 Studies
Andy Telfer
ISBN: 9781909919457

Making Work Work:
8 Studies
Marcus Nodder
ISBN: 9781908762894

The Holy Spirit: 8 Studies
Pete & Anne Woodcock
ISBN: 9781905564217

Experiencing God:
6 Studies
Tim Chester
ISBN: 9781906334437

Real Prayer: 7 Studies
Anne Woodcock
ISBN: 9781910307595

Mission: 7 Studies
Alan Purser
ISBN: 9781784983628

the good book

COMPANY

BIBLICAL | RELEVANT | ACCESSIBLE

At The Good Book Company, we are dedicated to helping Christians and local churches grow. We believe that God's growth process always starts with hearing clearly what he has said to us through his timeless word—the Bible.

Ever since we opened our doors in 1991, we have been striving to produce Bible-based resources that bring glory to God. We have grown to become an international provider of user-friendly resources to the Christian community, with believers of all backgrounds and denominations using our books, Bible studies, devotionals, evangelistic resources, and DVD-based courses.

We want to equip ordinary Christians to live for Christ day by day, and churches to grow in their knowledge of God, their love for one another, and the effectiveness of their outreach.

Call us for a discussion of your needs or visit one of our local websites for more information on the resources and services we provide.

Your friends at The Good Book Company

thegoodbook.com | thegoodbook.co.uk
thegoodbook.com.au | thegoodbook.co.nz
thegoodbook.co.in